Y0-ADY-490

Williamsburg
Jamestown
Yorktown
America's Historic Triangle

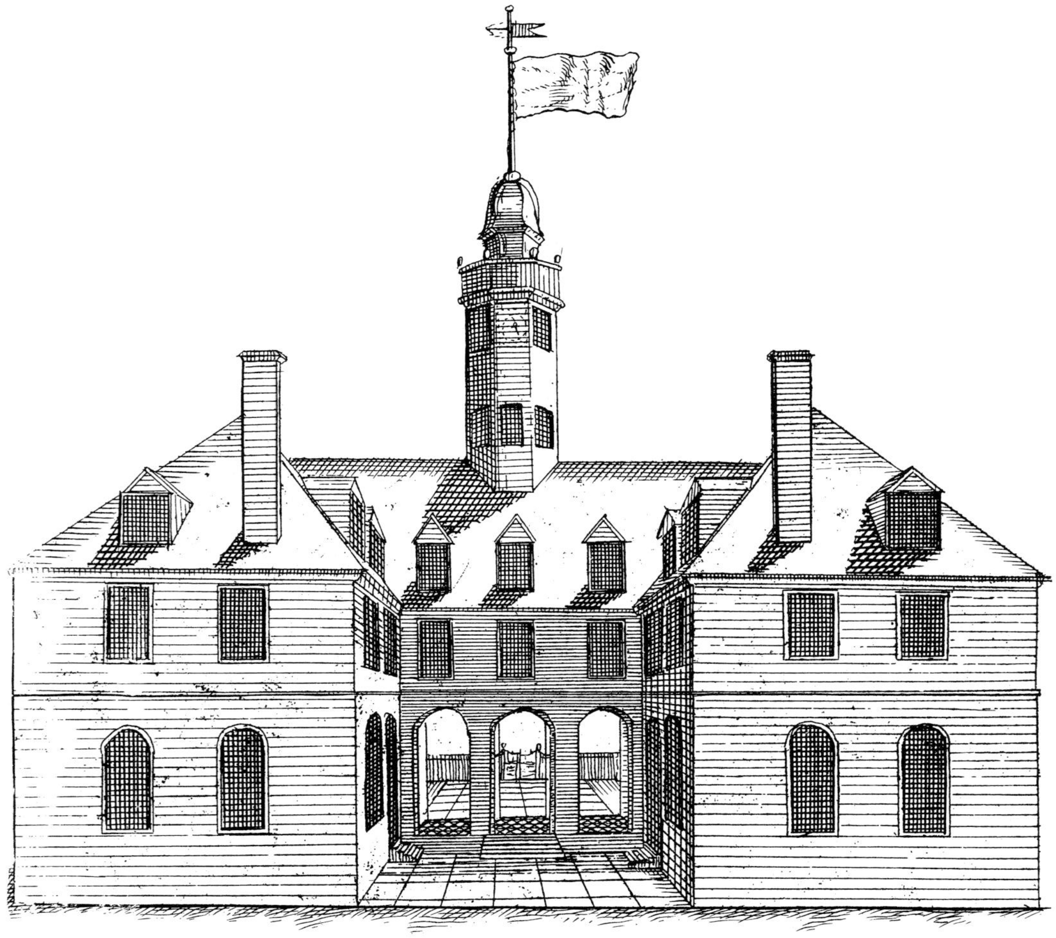

Williamsburg
~
Jamestown
~
Yorktown
~
America's Historic Triangle

PHOTOGRAPHY BY ROBERT LLEWELLYN

INTRODUCTION BY HUGH DESAMPER

UNIVERSE

The Publisher gratefully acknowledges the assistance of Cathy Grosfils, Mary Keeling, George Yetter, Richard McCluney, and other staff at the Colonial Williamsburg Foundation; Anne Marie Weissert and Debbie Padgett at the Jamestown-Yorktown Foundation; and Curt Gaul and Doug Thompson of the National Parks Service.

Frontispiece:
The Capitol, detail from *The Bodleian Plate*.
Photograph courtesy of the
Colonial Williamsburg Foundation

Published in the United States of America in 1995 by
UNIVERSE PUBLISHING
A division of Rizzoli International Publications, Inc.
300 Park Avenue South, New York, NY 10010

First published in the United States of America in 1991 by
Rizzoli International Publications, Inc.

No part of this publication may be reproduced in any manner whatsoever without permission in writing from Universe Publishing.

Copyright © 1991 Rizzoli International Publications
Photographs copyright © 1991 Robert Llewellyn
All rights reserved

Llewellyn, Robert, 1945–
Williamsburg, Jamestown, and Yorktown: America's historical triangle / photographs by Robert Llewellyn; introduction by Hugh DeSamper.
p. cm.
ISBN 0-8478-1405-X (Rizzoli HC edition)
ISBN 0-7893-0029-X (Universe HC edition)
1. Williamsburg (Va.)—Description—Views. 2. Jamestown (Va.)—
Description—Views. 3. Yorktown (Va.)—Description—Views.
4. Historic sites—Virginia—Williamsburg—Pictorial works.
5. Historic sites—Virginia—Jamestown—Pictorial works.
6. Historic sites—Virginia—Yorktown—Pictorial works.
I. DeSamper, Hugh. II. Title
F234.W7L55 1991
975.5'42—dc20   91-11423
                                                                CIP

Design by Gilda Hannah
Map by Lundquist Design, New York
Printed and bound in Singapore

CONTENTS

Introduction by Hugh DeSamper   7

WILLIAMSBURG   17

JAMESTOWN   119

YORKTOWN   145

Calendar of Annual Events   160

The Historic Triangle

Introduction

On May 13, 1607, three small English ships sailed up the James River carrying an assortment of adventurers, gentlemen, and fortune seekers. The group was charged with the establishment of a settlement in the New World and the generation of profits for its sponsor, the Virginia Company of London. After a difficult and discouraging start, marked by the alternate swelling of the population from resupply ships and its dwindling due to disease and famine, the fledgling colony began to expand across a peninsula bounded by broad rivers. Through the cultivation of tobacco supported by slave labor, the young colony gradually prospered.

More than a century and a half later, on the banks of the York River barely twenty miles from Jamestown, the Earl of Cornwallis and his British forces surrendered to an allied American and French army under General George Washington. Cornwallis later wrote that, having sustained severe damage and finding escape impossible, "I therefore proposed to capitulate." General Washington's victory in this climactic battle of the American Revolution made possible the forging of a new nation out of thirteen former colonies of Great Britain.

In the period between these two epic events, an economic, cultural, and political infrastructure evolved that was centered in Williamsburg, which succeeded Jamestown as the capital of Virginia in 1699. This thriving town encompassed a college, a church, a mansion for the royal governor, a capitol where two legislative bodies met to determine the affairs of Virginia, scores of taverns and ordinaries (inns), homes of the leading lights and struggling tradesmen, and an increasing number of indentured servants and slaves.

For nearly a century, events were focused in Williamsburg as it grew in size and importance. After midcentury, as the descendants of the first settlers found king and parliament ever more demanding and prone to taxation, patriots and statesmen here helped stoke the fires of insurrection. Yet, that revolutionary spirit, springing so early from Williamsburg, precipitated the city's decline. Desiring to be safer from enemy attack and nearer the center of population, the legislature moved the capital to Richmond in 1780—a severe blow to proud Williamsburg. Attention returned only briefly the next year as the armies, first of Cornwallis and then of Washington, passed through Williamsburg on their way to their fateful meeting on the high bluffs of Yorktown.

The Historic Triangle: Jamestown
England's interest in the New World had been mounting since the time of Sir Walter Raleigh's settlements at Roanoke Island. The defeat of the Spanish Armada in 1588 gave Britain new stature in the world order, greater safety on the seas, and a desire to expand her trade. But the interlocking alliances of the continent spurned Britain, and consequently she looked across the ocean. While colonization was too costly for an individual's resources, group-risk capital was available, and the Virginia Company of London was chartered on April 10, 1606. Ships were leased,

Site of Jamestown, On James River, Virginia, by Augustus Köllner, circa 1845. Pencil with pen and ink, and wash. Photograph courtesy of The New York Public Library.

settlers enlisted, supplies loaded, and instructions obtained from King James I and from the Virginia Company.

On December 20, 1606, the *Susan Constant* (100 tons and 79 feet at the waterline), the *Godspeed* (40 tons and about 50 feet), and the *Discovery* (20 tons and only 39 feet), sailed down the Thames River from London under the command of Captain Christopher Newport, bound for the New World. The 144 men aboard would be cramped, ill, disagreeable, and discouraged before the arduous voyage of five months came to an end. Straight off, the ships lay stranded along Britain's coast for weeks.

In his history of the voyage, colonist George Percy reported: "The fift of January we anchored in the Downes: but the winds continued contrarie so long, that we were forced to stay there some time, where we suffered great stormes, but . . . no great losse or danger." Finally, the winds shifted, and Captain Newport set a course that would take them to the Canary Islands, then across the Atlantic to the Virgin Islands, the Bahamas, and, in Percy's words, "into the Bay of Chesupioc" on April 26, 1607.

That same day the eager voyagers made a brief landing at Cape Henry among "faire meddowes and goodly tall trees, with such Fresh-waters running through the woods, as I was almost ravished at the first sight thereof." They also found spring flowers, oysters, and "fine beautiful strawberries." Here, and at the Indian village of Kecoughtan, they found natives. They were greeted at the former with bows and arrows and at the latter with food and dancing. After exploring the lower bay and nearby rivers for two weeks, Captain Newport moved his ships up the James River to an isthmus that was well protected and had good views up and down the river. On May 13, they landed after maneuvering so close to shore that they were "moored to the Trees in six fathom water."

The settlers exulted in their choice of this verdant, flower-covered site as their foothold in the New World. Crude huts and fortifications were started, and crops were planted. Percy wrote, "The fifteenth of June, we had built and finished our Fort, which was triangle-wise, having three Bulwarkes, at every corner, like a halfe Moone, and foure or five pieces of Artillerie mounted in them." Beyond each side of the fort was "a faire row of houses," and inside the triangular fort they built a church, a guardhouse, and a storehouse. "We had also sowne most of our Corne," Percy noted. "It sprang a mans height from the ground."

Once ashore, the settlers opened their orders from the Virginia Company, which named a seven-member council to govern the colony. Edward Maria Wingfield was elected president of the council. One of the seven, John Smith, was involved in a serious dispute during the voyage and ended up in irons. He was finally released and allowed to take his place on the council in early June.

Indians, principally about thirty Algonquin tribes that were part of a confederacy ruled by Chief Powhatan, were an early concern. One group attacked the fort in May, killing one and wounding eleven. Yet, in September, when the meager supplies of the colonists were nearly gone and half were already dead or dying of fever, friendly natives bearing "halfe ripe corn" brought them hope.

Smith, after his release from confinement, explored the Chesapeake and its tributaries for months, learning a great deal about the Indians, especially after being captured by Powhatan. "They are inconstant in everie thing," he wrote. "Craftie, timerous, quicke of apprehension and very ingenuous. Some are of disposition fearefull, some bold, some cautelous, all Savage. Generally covetous of copper, beads, and such like trash. They are soone moved to anger, and so malitious, that they seldome forget an injury."

Smith's analysis indicated that "the men be fewe; their far greater number is of women and children. Within 60 miles of James Towne there are about some 5000 people, but of able men fit for their warres scarse 1500."

The largest group of natives were the Chickahominy, numbering about one thousand, and located upriver from Jamestown. Smaller tribes were the Chiskiack on the York River, the Kecoughtan to the east near the bay, the Weanoc and Warrasqueoc on the south side of the James, and the Paspahegh and the Appomattoc, also upriver. With a few exceptions, the colonists found the natives friendly and helpful

Pocahontas. From the collection of the Jamestown-Yorktown Educational Trust.

at first, especially during the extended growing season. There was optimism amid the continuing hardships of life in an unknown and dangerous wilderness thousands of miles from their homeland.

The succeeding years, however, brought famine, fires, disease, dissension, Indian hatred, and massacres. The settlers quarreled among themselves frequently, and one man was sentenced to death and shot. The crops were doing poorly and the winter of 1609-1610 became known as "the starving time." The population, once as large as five hundred, fell off to only sixty. Finally, the surviving colonists boarded a ship and sailed away, abandoning the settlement.

Before they cleared the waters of Virginia, however, they met the *Virginia*, that had sailed from London bearing Lord Delaware, with new supplies and new settlers. Quickly, the refugees were persuaded—ordered, in fact, to return to Jamestown. In 1611 a force of three hundred men was sent up the James River to begin building the city of Henrico, marking the real beginning of an expansion that would be continuous, despite temporary setbacks.

Peace with the Indians came with the marriage in 1614 between John Rolfe and Pocahontas, and it lasted—at least for a while. In 1619 the first legislative assembly in the New World was created and the

Jamestown in 1622, from an early Dutch account of Virginia.

colonists were reintroduced to the same rights enjoyed by their British counterparts at home. That same year, a Dutch ship arrived with "20 and odd Negroes," which was the first step toward a system of slavery that was to develop in Virginia and other Southern colonies.

About this time, tobacco began to bring a degree of fame and stability to the colony, and more outposts, settlements, and plantations began to spring up along the rivers and even inland. Times were getting better.

Then, in 1622, a carefully planned Indian massacre struck many of the settlements and ended the peace. By this time the colonists were less prone to panic. They moved back within the fortifications of Jamestown and rode out the storm. Soon, a palisade was constructed across the peninsula, and an outpost called Middle Plantation was established. As the years passed, Jamestown—and Virginia—survived another massacre, the rule of Cromwell, a rebellion led by Nathaniel Bacon, and myriad fires.

Finally, in 1698, after fire destroyed Jamestown's fourth statehouse, many of the colony's legislators as well as Governor Francis Nicholson were ready for a change. The governor and the assembly, now obliged to meet in private homes, were discouraged by their misfortune. They were weary, too, of the low, acrid, swampy land, with its mosquitoes and attendant diseases. In early 1699, the assembly met at the home of Mrs. Sarah Lee and discussed finding a new location for their ill-fated capital.

They did find one, on higher ground midway across the peninsula, at the settlement called Middle Plantation. Governor Nicholson spoke fervently on behalf of the new site, claiming that "clear and crystal springs burst from champagne soil." The fact that Jamestown was home to malaria and mosquitoes bolstered his argument. With the founding of a new capital—named Williamsburg in honor of King William III—Jamestown was all but abandoned. It was an ignominious end to a bold and successful experiment, one that brought fame and fortune to many of its inhabitants, as well as to England.

The Historic Triangle: Williamsburg

Governor Nicholson threw himself into the task of creating a new capital, and the assembly, on June 7, 1699, passed a "Bill directing the Building of the Capitol and the City of Williamsburg." Two hundred twenty acres were surveyed and allotted to the city, with additional land on nearby creeks, to be named Queen Marys Port and Princess Ann Port. At that time Middle Plantation consisted of "a Church, an Ordinary, several Stores, two Mills, a smiths shop a Grammar School, and above all the Colledge." An old horseway was its main street. The site presented a superior opportunity to develop a well-ordered city on a completely new plan.

Francis Nicholson supervised the design. The new principal street, named for William, Duke of Gloucester, began at the college and stretched a mile to the east, where the capitol was built. The town plan included two streets parallel to the principal avenue—which the governor modestly named Francis and Nicholson Streets—and numerous other streets in a grid pattern. The assembly's bill also directed that the city be separated into half-acre lots and that "whosoever shall build in the maine Street . . . shall not build a House less than tenn Foot Pitch and the Front of each House shall come within six Foot of the Street and not nearer and that the Houses in the severall Lots in the said main Street shall front a like."

Edward Nott succeeded Nicholson as governor in 1705 and, although the assembly had resisted this for some time, secured passage in 1706 of "An Act directing the Building an House for the Governor." About halfway between the college and capitol, a north-south axis was created, with a long green leading north to the site for the governor's residence. Governor Nott never saw his house, for he died that same year. When Governor Alexander Spotswood arrived in 1710, the building was under construction but was lagging, and he set himself to see it to completion. It appears that he was overzealous, for the minutes of the House of Burgesses of November 21, 1718, state that the governor "lavishes away the Country's Money contrary to the Intent of the Law." Eventually, Governor Spotswood contributed some of his own funds to help complete the growing complex, but this did not prevent someone from dubbing it "the Palace," a name which it retains today.

When completed in 1722, the royal residence was hailed as one of the finest in the colonies. The governor's house, the capitol, and the college—all built of brick—comprised an orderly ensemble that made a handsome start for the city. The new metropolis grew in several directions. Around the Palace Green were several modest, one-and-a-half-story houses, a tavern, a theater, and several craftsmen's shops. Guests of the governor saw piles of coal that gunsmith James Geddy used at his forge and foundry, and in later years a lead manufactory and a coachworks were established behind houses facing on the Green.

In many respects, the Palace Green was the center of the cultural life of Williamsburg. Of considerable importance was William Levingston's playhouse, which was constructed in 1716 and was the first theater in the American colonies. In 1718 Governor Spotswood celebrated the first play known to have been performed at the theater. While the upper class frequented the playhouse, it was also a source of enjoyment for many of lower status. The playhouse was often boisterous and rowdy, with catcalls, arguments, and flying fruit. But the theater was nevertheless a civilizing influence, as citizens learned a bit

Portrait of Governor Spotswood by Charles Bridges, circa 1735-40. Photograph courtesy of Colonial Williamsburg Foundation.

about socially acceptable behavior while absorbing the comedy and satire of the day.

Virginia's eighteenth-century royal governors were generally considered capable and amicable, and they entertained frequently and sometimes lavishly.

In November, 1752, *The Virginia Gazette* reported: "Friday last, being the Anniversary of his Majesty's Birth-Day, in the Evening, the whole City was illuminated. There was a Ball, and a very elegant Entertainment, at the Palace, where were present, the Emperor and Empress of the Cherokee Nation, with their Son the young Prince, and a brilliant appearance of Ladies and Gentlemen; several beautiful Fireworks were exhibited in Palace Street, by Mr. Hallam manager of the Theatre in this City."

As the revolution neared, clashes between the House of Burgesses and the governor became more frequent. Still, the governors were respected and popular, particularly Fauquier (1758–68) and Botetourt (1768–70), despite the colonists' growing distress with the parliament and the king.

During the periods of "Publick Times" in the spring and fall, when the general court and often the assembly met, the city was thronged with visitors.

The Bodleian Plate showing eighteenth-century drawings of some of Williamsburg's main buildings. They are from the left, top: the Brafferton, the Wren Building, and the President's House at the college. Middle, from the left: the Capitol, the back of the Wren Building, and the Governor's Palace. Bottom: a Virginia Indian and flora and fauna. Photograph courtesy of the Colonial Williamsburg Foundation.

Burgesses came in from the plantations and frontier towns with their families, and other Virginians came to conduct business, meet with friends, and talk politics. The days and nights were filled with music, dance, and theater, as well as the announced events of the season. In April, 1765, a French traveller recorded his reactions: "I got a room at mrs. vaube's tavern, where all the best people resorted. I soon got acquainted with severals of them . . . which I soon was like to have had reason to repent, for they are all professed gamesters, Especially Colonel Burd, who is never happy but when he has the box and Dices in Hand." The same diarist also observed: "In the Day time people hurying back and forwards from the Capitoll to the taverns, and at night, Carousing and Drinking in one Chamber and box and Dice in another, which Continues till morning Commonly. There is not a publick house in virginia but have their tables all baterd with the boxes which shews the Extravagant Disposition of the planters; there are many of them who have very great Estates, but are mostly at loss for Cash."

It has been said that the "ball of revolution" gained its first impulse in 1765, from Patrick Henry in Williamsburg. In the capitol on his twenty-ninth birthday, Henry, a legislator representing Louisa County, introduced a set of resolves condemning the Stamp Act. The following day, five of his resolves were passed, after, according to Thomas Jefferson, a "most bloody" debate. On May 31, after Henry had left for home, the conservative burgesses rescinded the fifth and most controversial resolution, but the news had already been dispatched to the other colonies, and the resolves fueled a storm that led to the eventual repeal of the unpopular tax.

According to *The Virginia Gazette*, the repeal caused "a Ball and elegant Entertainment" to be held at the capitol, "at which was present His Honour the

A Williamsburg street before 1921. Photograph courtesy of the Colonial Williamsburg Foundation.

Governor [Fauquier], many of the Members of his Majesty's Council, and a large and genteel Company of Ladies and Gentlemen, who spent the Evening with much Mirth and Decorum, and drank all the loyal and patriotick Toasts."

Virginia's last royal governor was John Murray, the fourth Earl of Dunmore. He had been governor of New York for less than a year when he was appointed, at an increase in salary, to succeed the recently deceased Lord Botetourt as governor of Virginia. His reaction was explosive: "Damn Virginia. Did I ever seek it? Why is it forced upon me? I ask'd for New York—New York I took, and they have robbed me of it without my consent." This was inauspicious news to the people of Williamsburg, and the relationship generally went downhill from there.

The "ball of revolution" soon became a fixture in the streets of Williamsburg. On April 21, 1775, British Marines, acting on orders from Governor Dunmore, removed the colonists' gunpowder from the Magazine and transferred it to a warship in the James River. This incident festered for ten days or more before the governor authorized payment for the stolen powder. By early June the news of Concord, Lexington, and other skirmishes had reached Williamsburg, and Governor Dunmore thought it wise to evacuate his seat. On June 8, he and his family left the city in the dead of night for the safety of the frigate *Fowey* at Yorktown.

Lady Dunmore and her children sailed for home before the month was out, and her departure was mourned by the populace. A letter published in *The Virginia Gazette* observed, "Your illustrious character fills the breast of Virginia with love and admiration . . . Had your lord possessed half the engaging qualities that embellish your mind . . . he would have been the idol of a brave and free people and not drawn upon himself their detestation."

Activity intensified in Williamsburg, which had become a training ground—and a proving ground—for many of the future patriots, statesmen, and military leaders of the new nation. In the spring of 1776,

Portrait of Patrick Henry by Thomas Sully, circa 1815. Photograph courtesy of the Colonial Williamsburg Foundation.

the Virginia Convention of Delegates gathered at the capitol for a session that was to be of historic significance. On May 15, the convention unanimously adopted the Virginia Resolution for Independence, which called on Virginians attending the Continental Congress in Philadelphia to propose independence and union for all the colonies. The glorious July 4th Declaration of Independence, announcing a new member in the community of independent nations, was a direct result of this act. On June 12, the convention passed George Mason's Declaration of Rights, which formed much of the basis for the Federal Bill of Rights. Finally, on June 29, the convention adopted a new constitution for the free Commonwealth of Virginia and elected Patrick Henry the new governor.

Thomas Jefferson succeeded Patrick Henry as governor of Virginia on June 1, 1779. Within a few days, a proposal to move the seat of government to Richmond, which was "more safe and central than any other Town situated on navigable Water," was adopted by the General Assembly. On March 25, 1780, *The Virginia Gazette* noted, "the Business of Government, in the Executive Department, will cease to be transacted at Williamsburg from the 7th of April next, and will commence at Richmond on the 24th of the same Month."

The transfer of the capital marked the close of another epoch in the life of Williamsburg. For more than a century it had been the heart and center of the Commonwealth. Even as new cities began to match or exceed it in area and population, Williamsburg, until the departure of the capital, was a giant among them in influence and accomplishment. For as Jamestown, when it was the capital, steered Virginia through the perils of settlement and conquest, Williamsburg, in its years, successfully led the colony through decades of stabilization and expansion, and charted the course for liberty.

The Historic Triangle: Yorktown

The war did not go well. The Continental Army was poorly clad and fed, and seldom paid, and yet it fought bravely and often brilliantly under the leadership of General Washington. Victories, few and scattered, came just often enough to prevent a collapse of the Union. With French aid came new hope in the form of regiments led by Lafayette and Rochambeau and a fleet under Admiral DeGrasse. In the spring of 1781, the British commander Lord Cornwallis mounted a southern campaign designed to split Washington's forces. Slowly, the trail led to Yorktown, some twelve miles from Williamsburg and about twenty from Jamestown. Here, the points of the triangle were connected forever with the surrender of the British on October 19, 1781.

Epilogue: The Twentieth Century

In modern America, the Historic Triangle provides the visitor with a substantive, retrospective experience of the three principal elements of Virginia and the nation. Optimally, the points of the triangle should be seen in chronological order.

First, Jamestown Island is preserved and presented by the National Parks Service and the Association for the Preservation of Virginia Antiquities. Here, examples of the wilderness of 1607, brick foundations from as early as 1622, excavated remains of three of the four statehouses, various remnants from the old town site, and the ruins of the 1639 church tower stimulate the imagination and prompt one to look for Indians in a grove of nearby trees. The Visitor Center presents a scholarly selection of exhibits, maps, dioramas, and models, as well as monuments.

Yorktown: Surrender of Cornwallis, circa 1781. Hand-colored line engraving. Photograph courtesy of the Colonial Williamsburg Foundation.

A drive along an established historical route on the island provides tranquility, additional information, and an impression of the natural beauty that greeted the settlers nearly four centuries ago.

Another vital part of the Jamestown experience is the Jamestown Settlement, where the colonists' three ships, the fort, and the church and other buildings have been replicated and are operated by the Commonwealth of Virginia. Artifacts, documents, and exhibits in newly expanded and remodeled museum galleries present the Jamestown story graphically and imaginatively. The full-scale reproductions of the *Susan Constant*, the *Godspeed*, and the *Discovery*, reminders of that first, fateful trans-Atlantic voyage in the winter of 1607, are extremely popular. In the fort and nearby Indian village, visitors observe the ways of life during those early, struggling years. It is impossible to leave this site without marveling at the courage, strength, and perseverance of the people who wrote the first chapter of our nation's history.

For the second point of the triangle, visitors should plan at least two full days to tour the Historic Area of Williamsburg—173 acres of the original 1699 town plan, including nearly ninety surviving buildings—which is preserved and interpreted by the Colonial Williamsburg Foundation. Open every day in every season, Colonial Williamsburg offers an impressive slate of opportunities to touch the past. On the mile-long Duke of Gloucester Street, coaches and carts rumble past, a fife and drum corps parades, costumed housewives hurry on their shopping rounds, businessmen and legislators discuss the issues of the day, and servants and slaves carry out their duties.

Inside the many places of exhibition, historical interpreters take visitors back in time. In the original home of Peyton Randolph, the respected president of the First Continental Congress, one can imagine being there in August, 1774, as Randolph read Jefferson's first important Williamsburg document, "A Summary View of the Rights of British America." A visitor is able to debate the issues of the Stamp Act in the capitol during an evening program of participatory interpretation. One can observe the gunsmith, the wheelwright, the shoemaker, the silversmith, and two dozen other kinds of tradesmen as they demonstrate and preserve the hand methods of the master workmen of the 1770s. The original home of lawyer and professor George Wythe is open to inspection, where Washington, Lafayette, and Rochambeau planned the climactic Yorktown campaign. Behind the fine brick home, many of the domestic duties of the period may be observed in the outbuildings.

One can visit the Governor's Palace during the day as the colony's business takes place and return in the evening for a concert or ball. The newly restored Courthouse offers insight into 1770s justice, and a stage at the site of the first theater in America presents the period's wry and comic scenes. The militia—citizen soldiers—drills on Market Square Green.

Williamsburg's inns, taverns, and ordinaries were filled to overflowing at Publick Times. Today, visitors may rent a room at the Market Square Tavern and take a meal across the Duke of Gloucester Street at Josiah Chowning's Tavern or at Mrs. Campbell's Tavern on the Capitol Exchange. Businessman John Greenhow discusses merchandising and economics at his store, and a few blocks away at Mr. Prentis's store, there may be word of tea thrown overboard at Yorktown in Virginia's own version of the Boston Tea Party.

In the spring, the flowering trees and shrubs, and the tulips and other colorful blossoms, cheer the eye and hearten the spirit. In the summer, full outdoor activity complements the indoor programs. In the fall, beginning with the thronging Publick Times of Labor Day weekend (with its Market Days, street hawkers, auctions, encampments of Continental Army units and British regulars, and other entertainments), a season of cultural events is capped by a brilliant palette of red, gold, and orange, backed by evergreen, as the deciduous maples, oaks, and dogwoods follow the dictates of nature and prepare for winter. December brings a month of Christmas filled with balls, theater, assemblies, caroling, militia and fife and drum parades, and feasting, against a backdrop of sparkling doorway decorations on every colonial building. It all begins with a lively "Grand Illumination of the City," when fireworks light up the heavens in the spirit of the "King's Birth-Night" celebrations. Each night during the season candles illuminate the windows and cupolas of the Historic Area, and there are periodic evening programs of a *son et lumière* nature to add excitement. After the new year, scholarly and educational programs prevail, including the annual Antiques Forum, Learning Weekend, several Colonial Weekends, and special lectures.

Finally, the battlefield, the redoubts, and the surrender field where Cornwallis's troops lay down their arms, and the eighteenth-century Moore House where the Articles of Capitulation were drawn up and signed, present an opportunity to capture vivid images of a turning point in American history. The Visitor Center, operated by the National Parks Service, and the Victory Center, operated by the Commonwealth of Virginia, both offer fascinating exhibits.

The colonial National Historical Parkway, a limited-access, low-speed federal byway, extends from Jamestown to Williamsburg to Yorktown, and in the spring it is spectacular. Beginning in late March, the greenery lining the parkway is smothered with dogwood and redbud. It alone is worth the trip for some.

Hugh DeSamper
Williamsburg, Virginia

Williamsburg

Upon the whole, [Williamsburg] is an agreeable residence; there are ten or twelve gentlemen's families constantly residing in it, besides merchants and tradesmen: and at the times of the assemblies, and general courts, it is crowded with the gentry of the country: on those occasions there are balls and other amusements; but as soon as the business is finished, they return to their plantations; and the town is in a manner deserted.

~ Reverend Andrew Burnaby, 1759-60

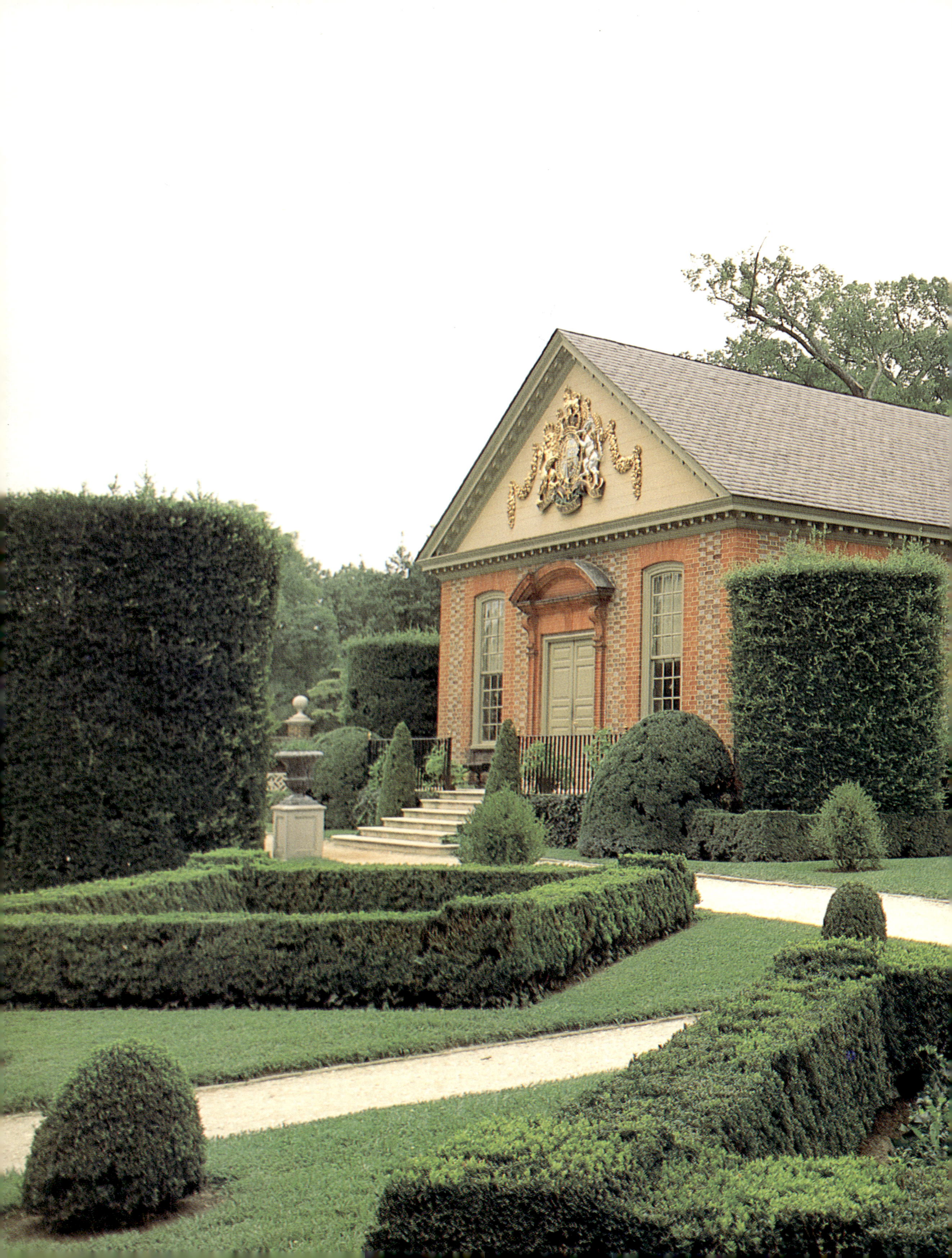

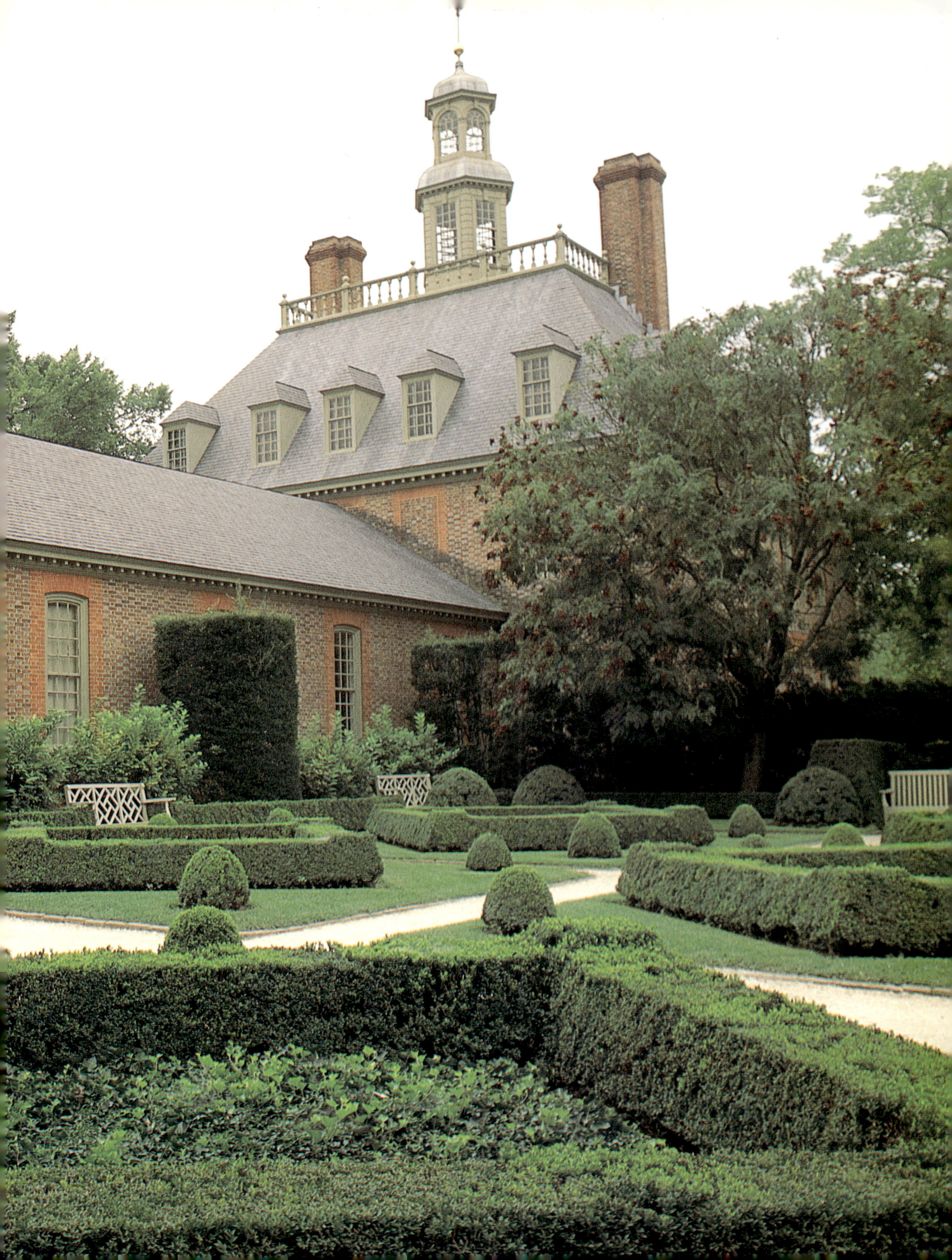

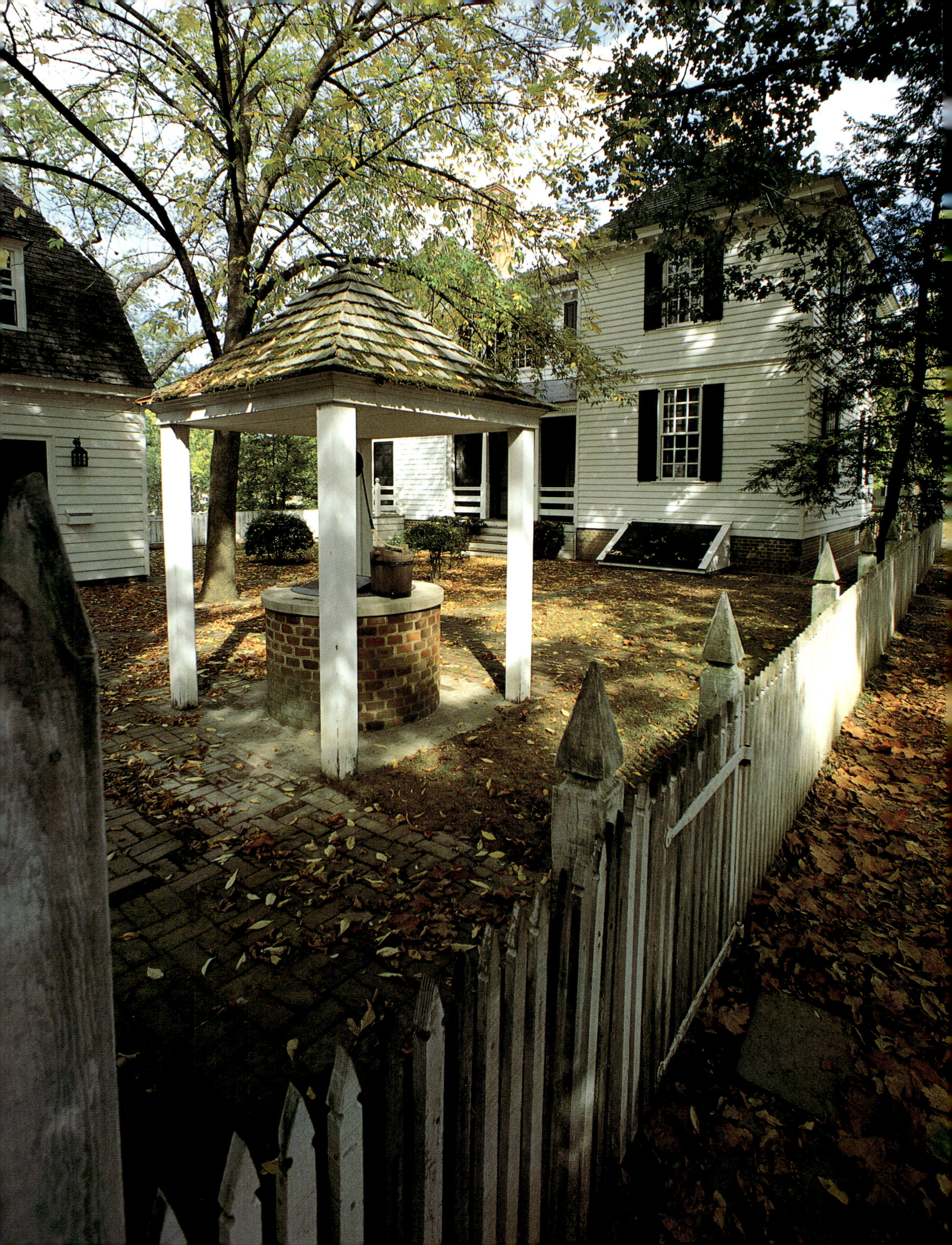

Pages 18 and 19: The Governor's Palace seen from the Ballroom Garden. The Palace was the residence of seven royal governors and the first two governors of the Commonwealth of Virginia—Patrick Henry and Thomas Jefferson.

Opposite: The gardens of the Elkanah Deane House on Prince George Street. The house is a reconstruction of the original 1761 structure.

A milkmaid strolls on the Palace Green.

Pages 22 and 23: An aerial view of Colonial Williamsburg.

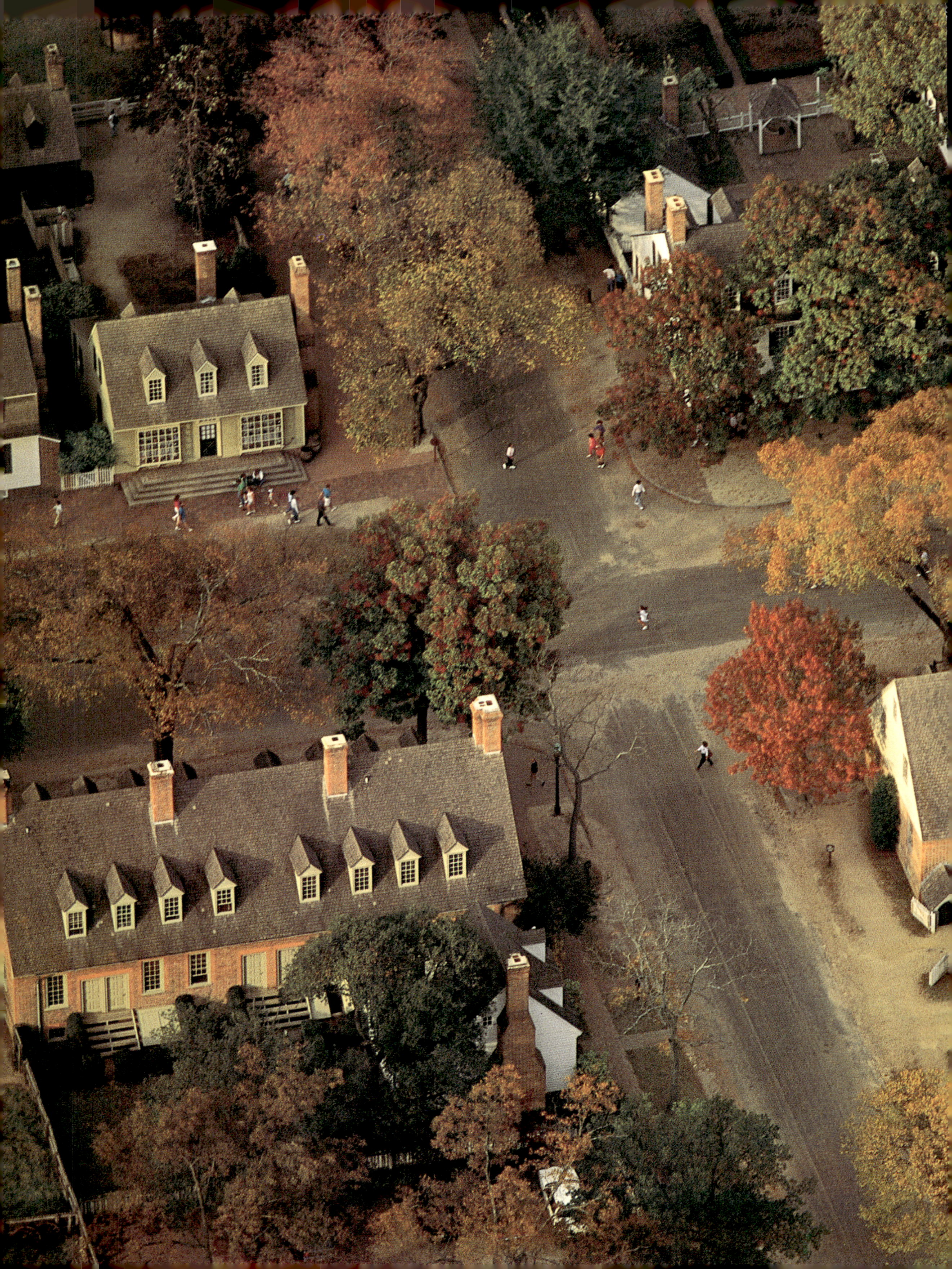

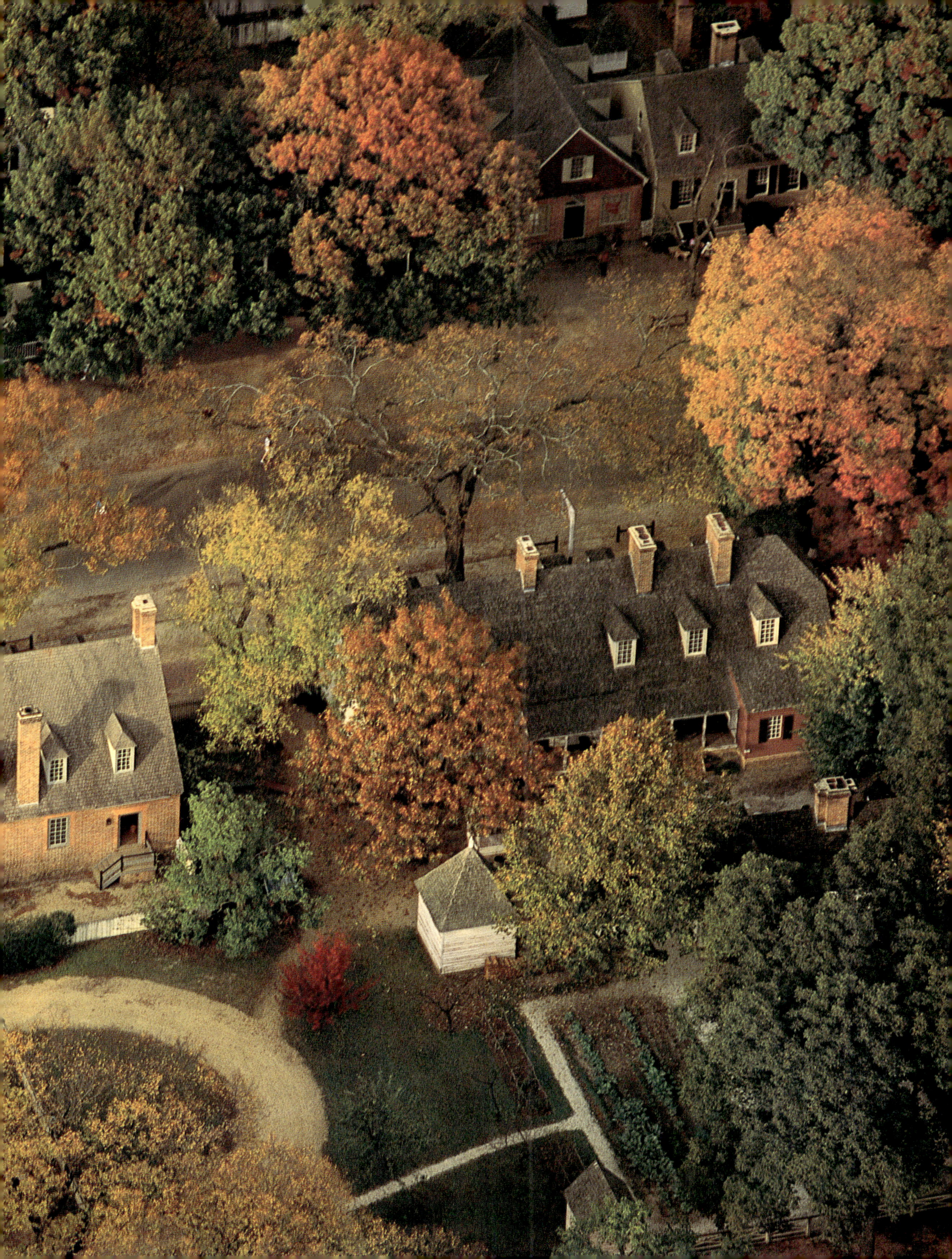

Robertson's Windmill on North England Street is a copy of the original 1723 windmill.

The gardens of the George Wythe House on Palace Street. This historic house, dated 1752-54, was used by George Washington as headquarters during the Yorktown Campaign.

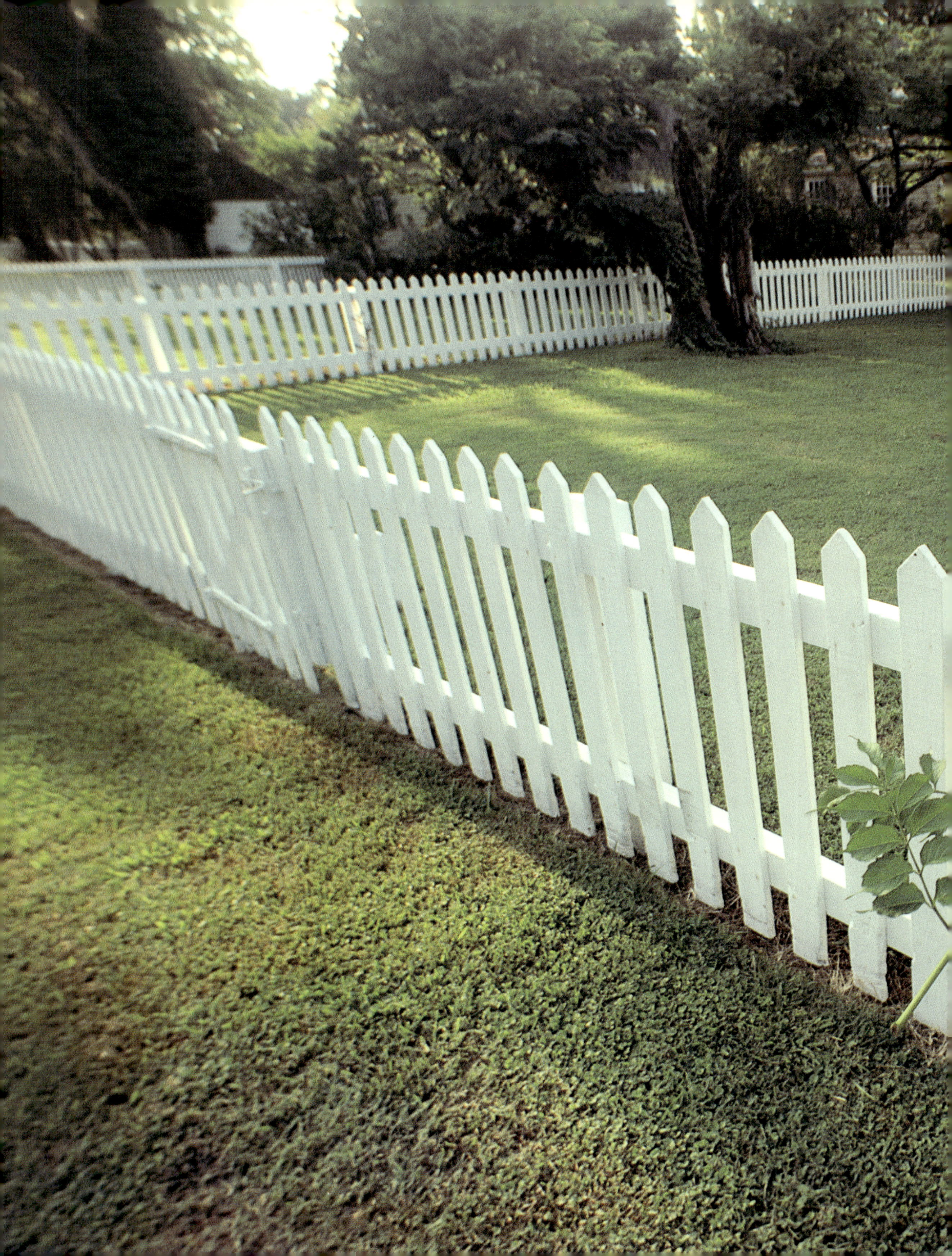

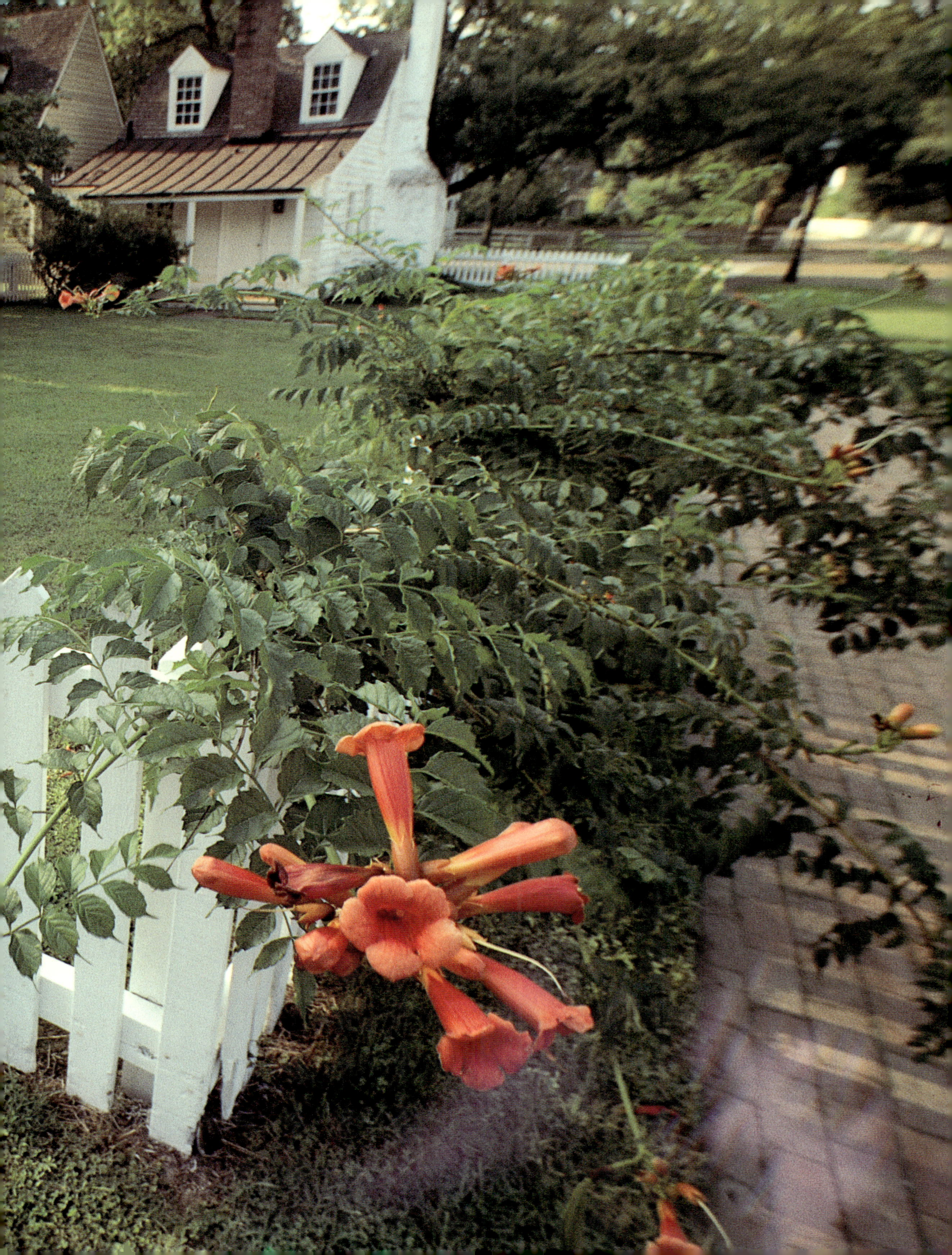

~

Williamsburg is the capital of Virginia…It is regularly laid out in parallel streets, intersected by others at right angles; has a handsome square in the center, through which runs the principal street, one of the most spacious in North-America, three quarters of a mile in length, and above a hundred feet wide. At the ends of this street are two public buildings, the college and the capitol.

Reverend Andrew Burnaby, 1759-60

Pages 26 and 27: Picket fence along Francis Street.

Opposite: A horse and cart trundles across the Palace Green.

Pages 30 and 31: Tarpley's Store as it might have looked in 1775.

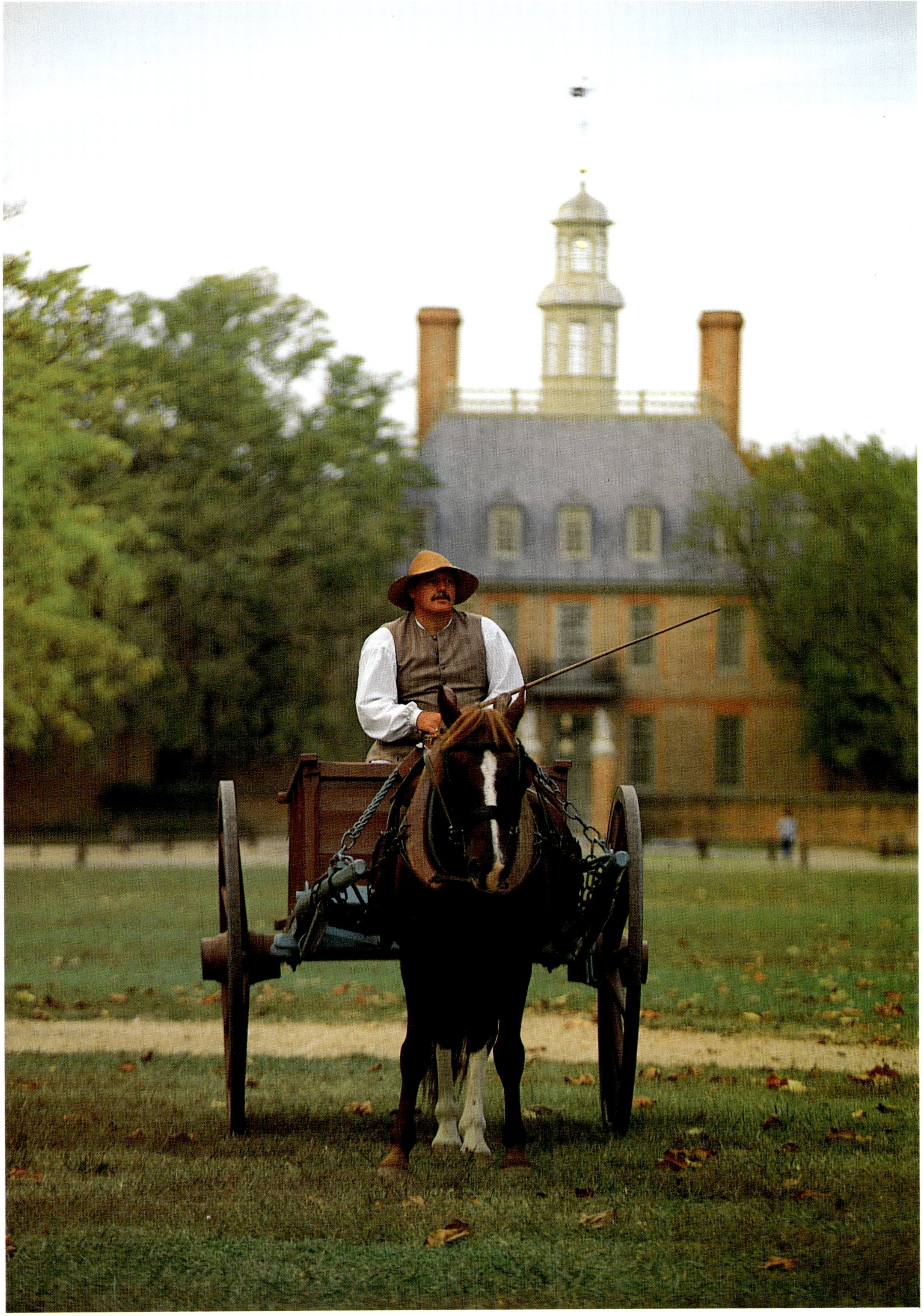

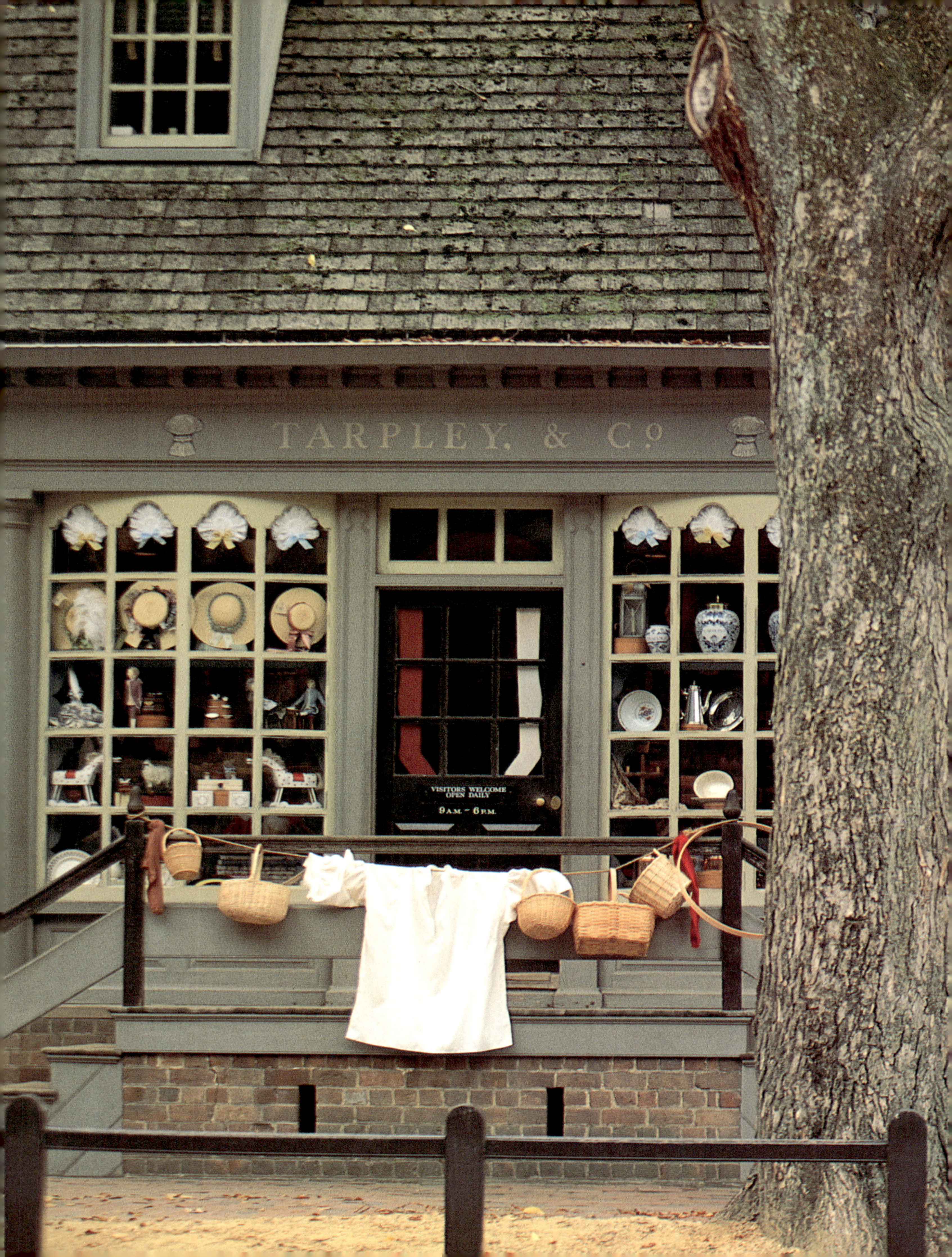
TARPLEY, & C°
VISITORS WELCOME
OPEN DAILY
9 A.M. - 6 P.M.

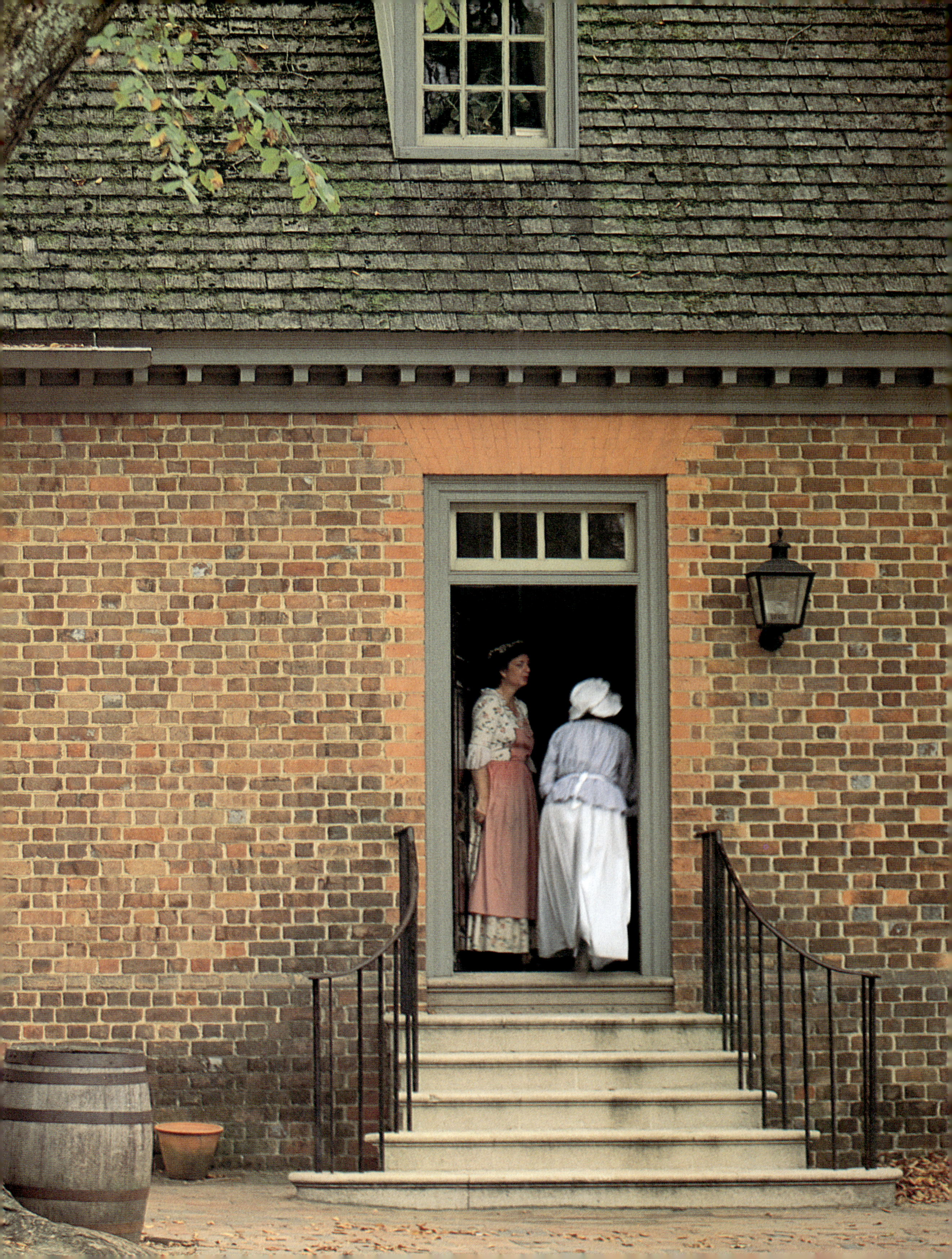

Wigs in the King's Arms barbershop. This business concern was first mentioned in *The Virginia Gazette* in 1768. The sign reads: "Barber and Peruke Maker" (wig maker).

Shop windows on the Duke of Gloucester Street showing fine silverware and china, just as in colonial days.

Pages 34 and 35: Children frolic in the garden behind the historic James Geddy House.

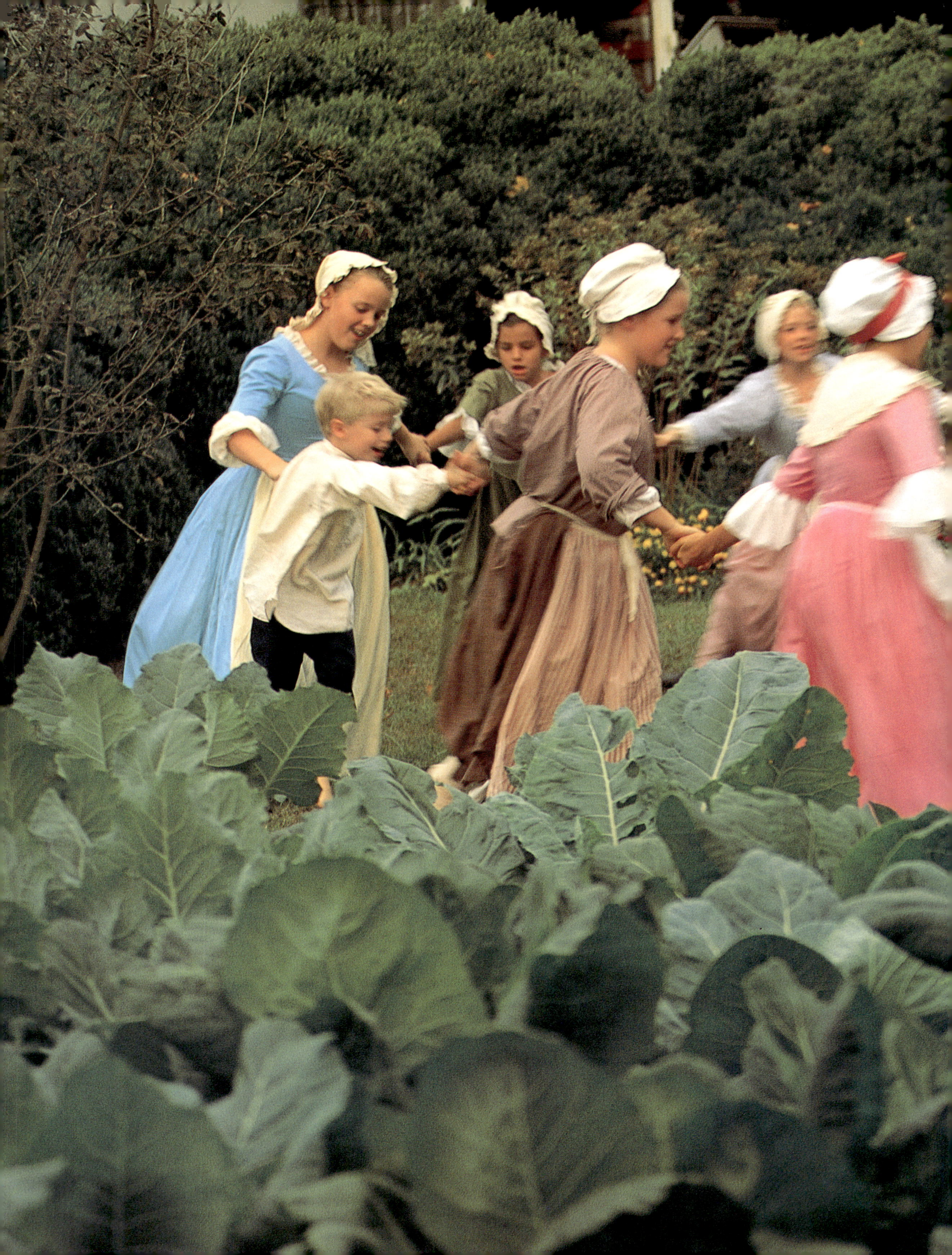

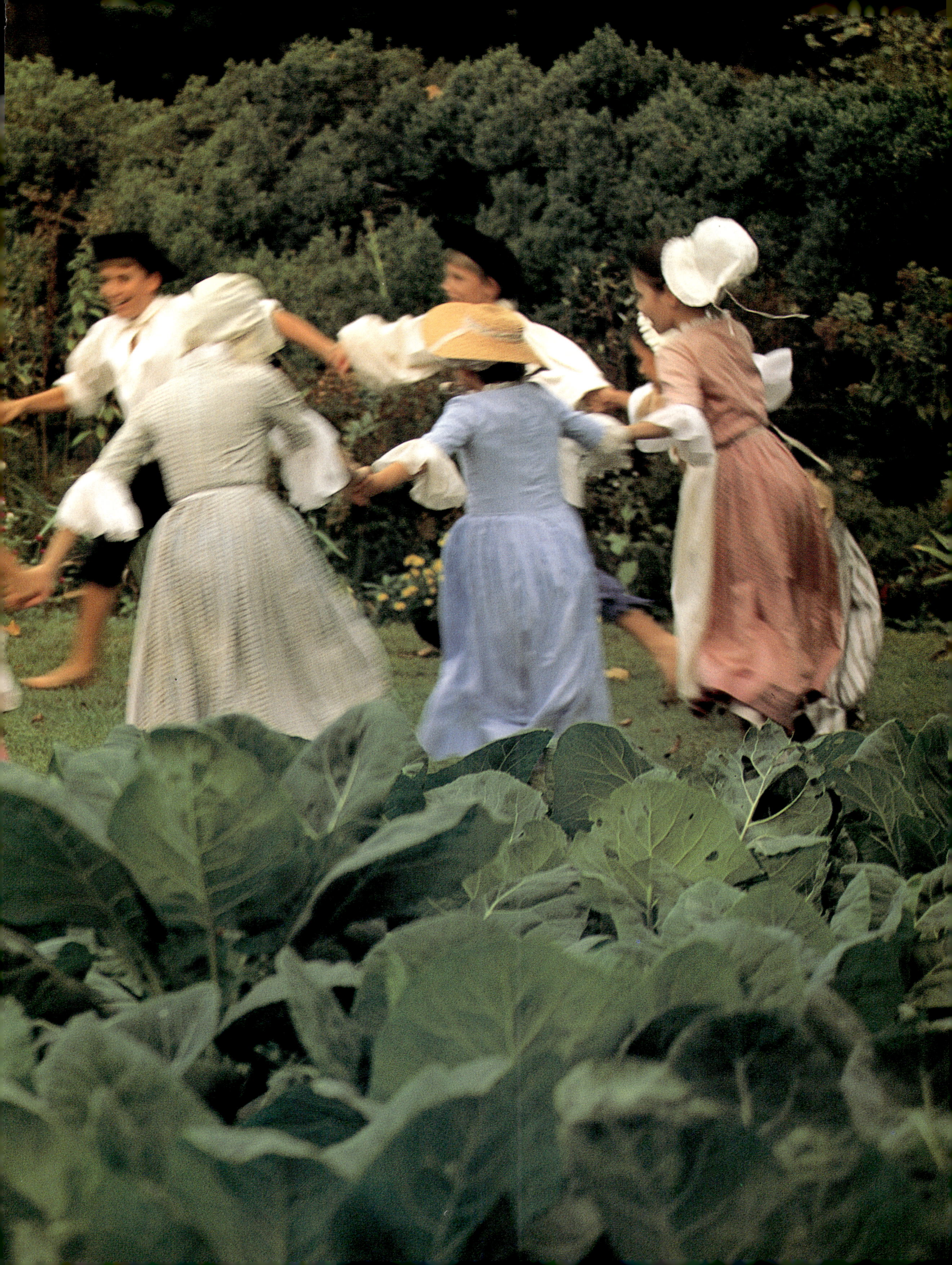

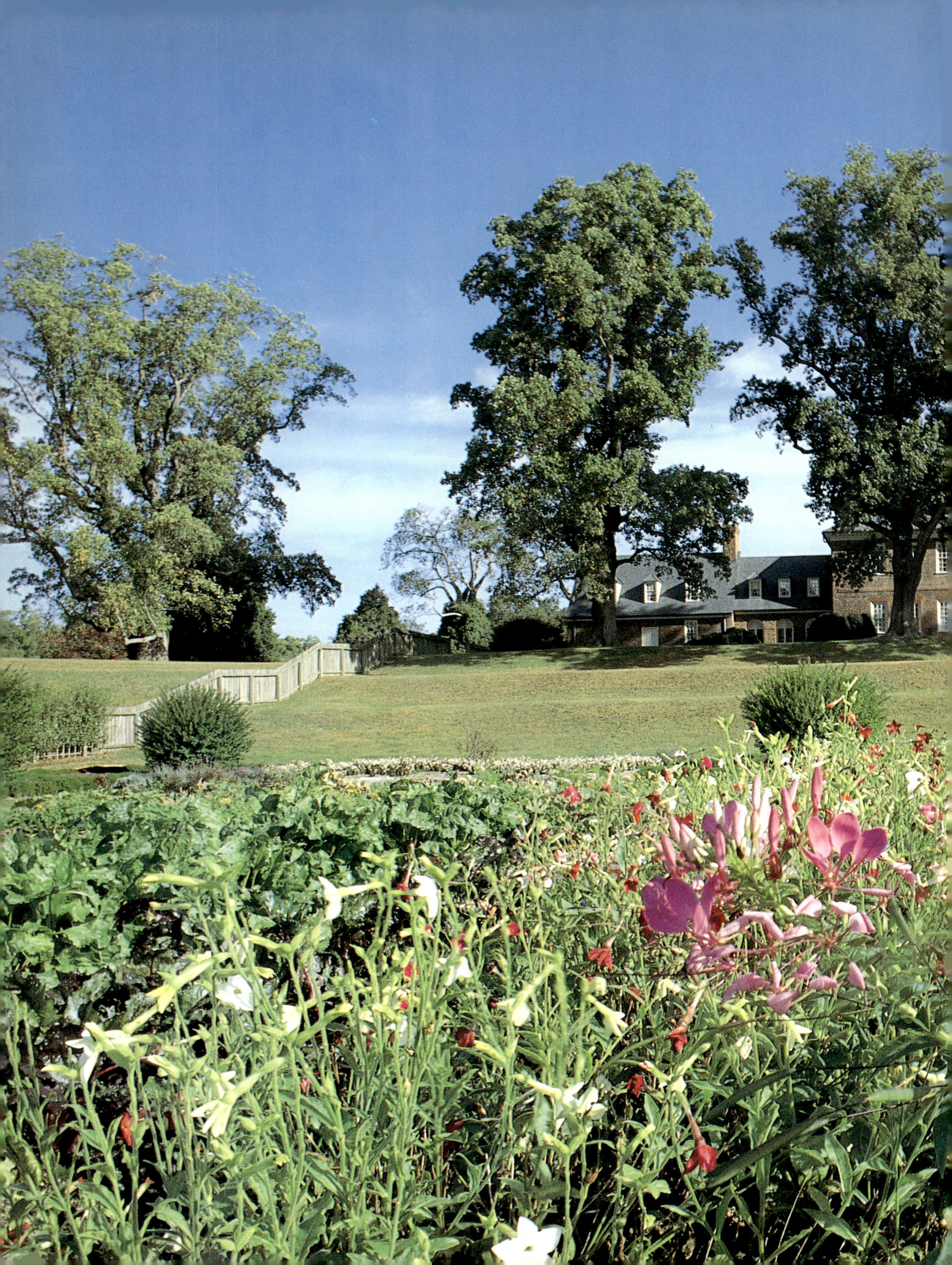

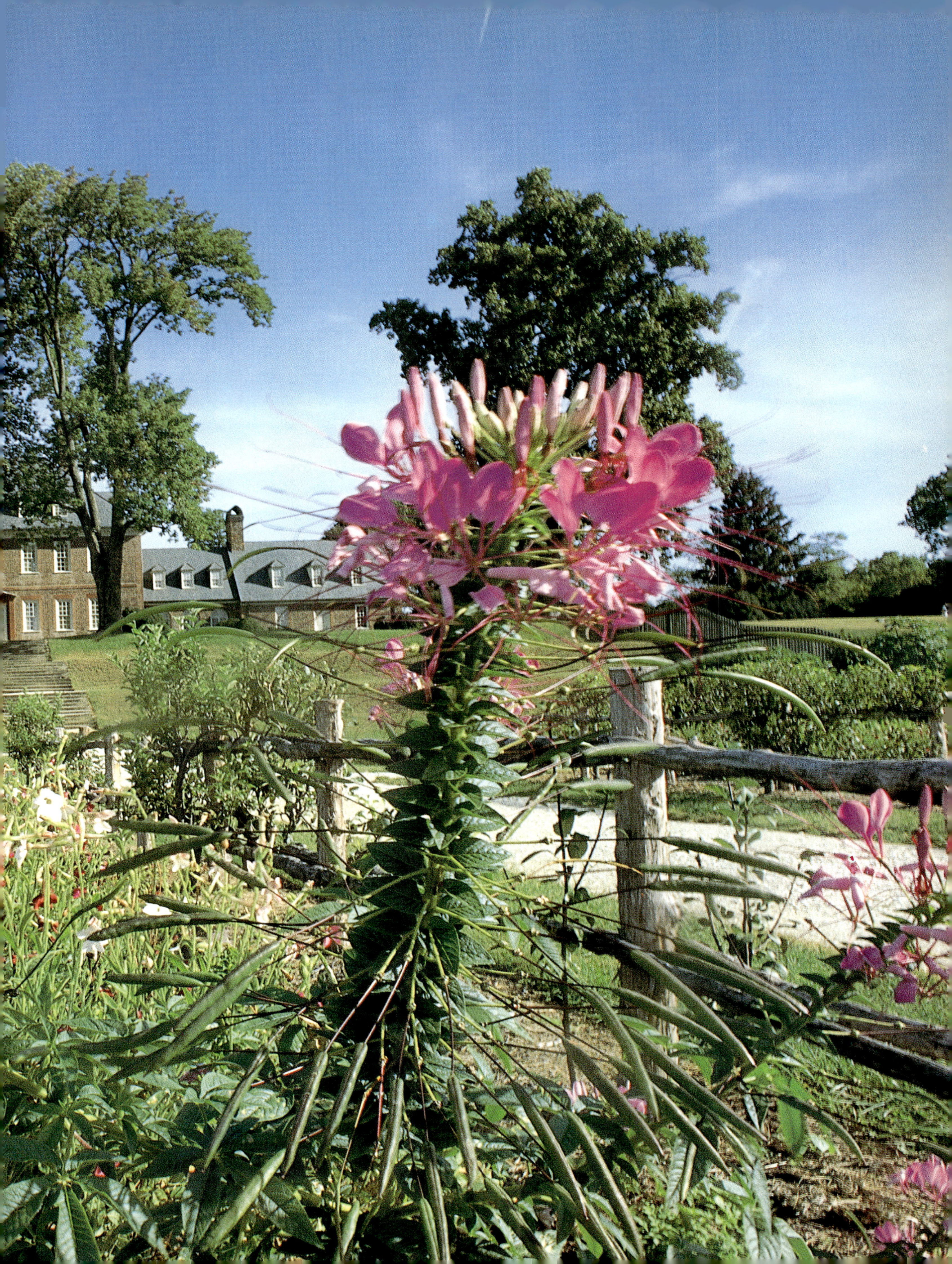

∼

Last Friday being the Anniversary of our most gracious Sovereign's Accession to the Throne, his Excellency the Governour gave a Ball and an elegant Entertainment at the Palace, to a numerous and splendid Company of Ladies and Gentlemen. The Raleigh Tavern likewise, by Direction of his Excellency, was opened for the Entertainment of Such as might incline to spend the Evening there; plenty of Liquor was given to the Populace; and the City was handsomely illuminated.

The Virginia Gazette
Williamsburg, October 31, 1771

Pages 36 and 37: The gardens and mansion at Carter's Grove Plantation, built between 1750 and 1755 by Carter Burwell.

Opposite: The front gate of the Governor's Palace as it would have appeared in the mid-eighteenth century.

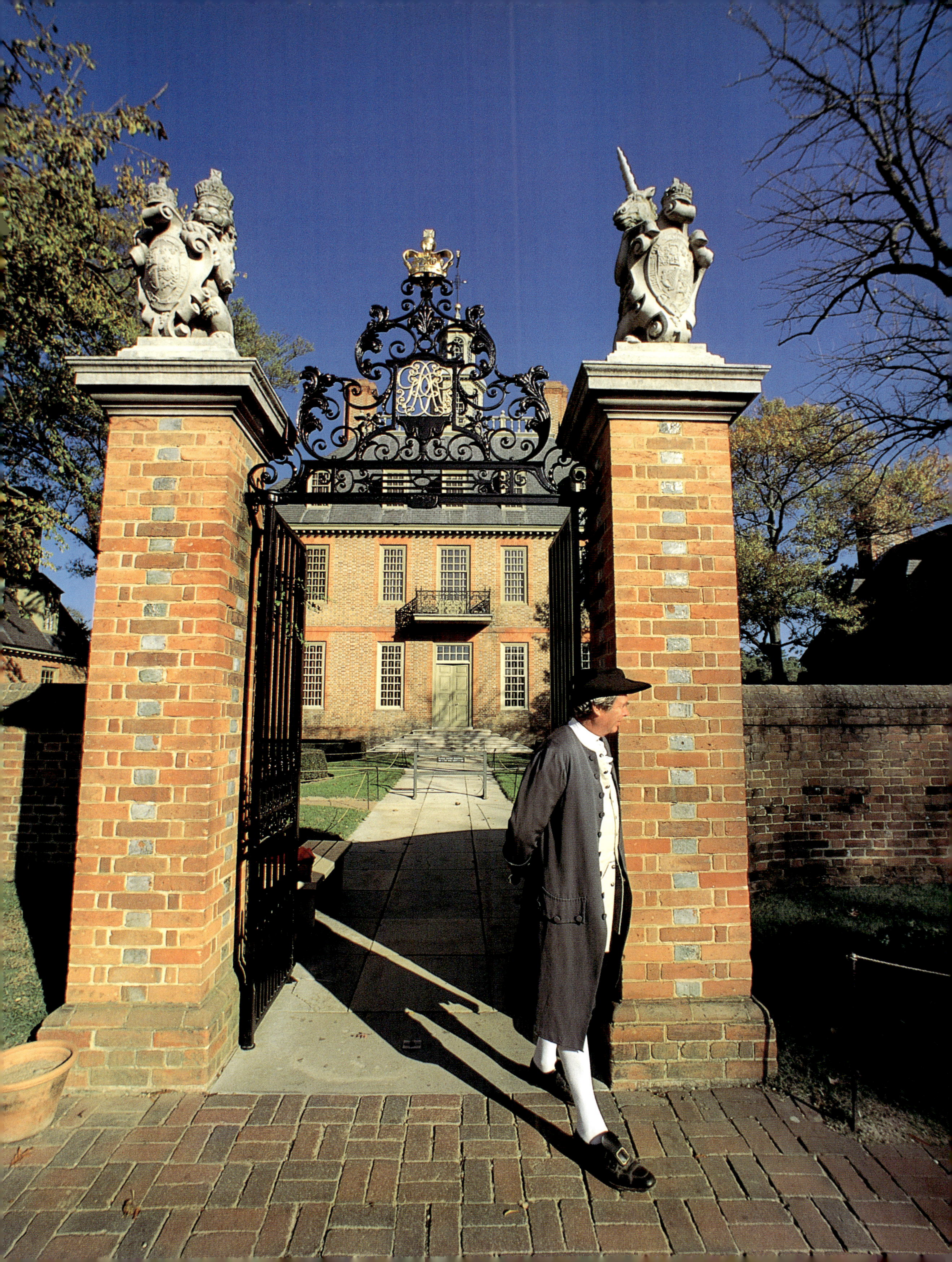

Christmas in Williamsburg at the Peyton Randolph House, built in mid-eighteenth century. The custom at Christmas was to deck the houses and churches with boughs of ivy, bay, and other evergreens.

Opposite: Christmas dinner in colonial times would have consisted of chowders, roast turkey, Virginia ham, spoon bread and corn sticks, pecan pie, and the wassail bowl.

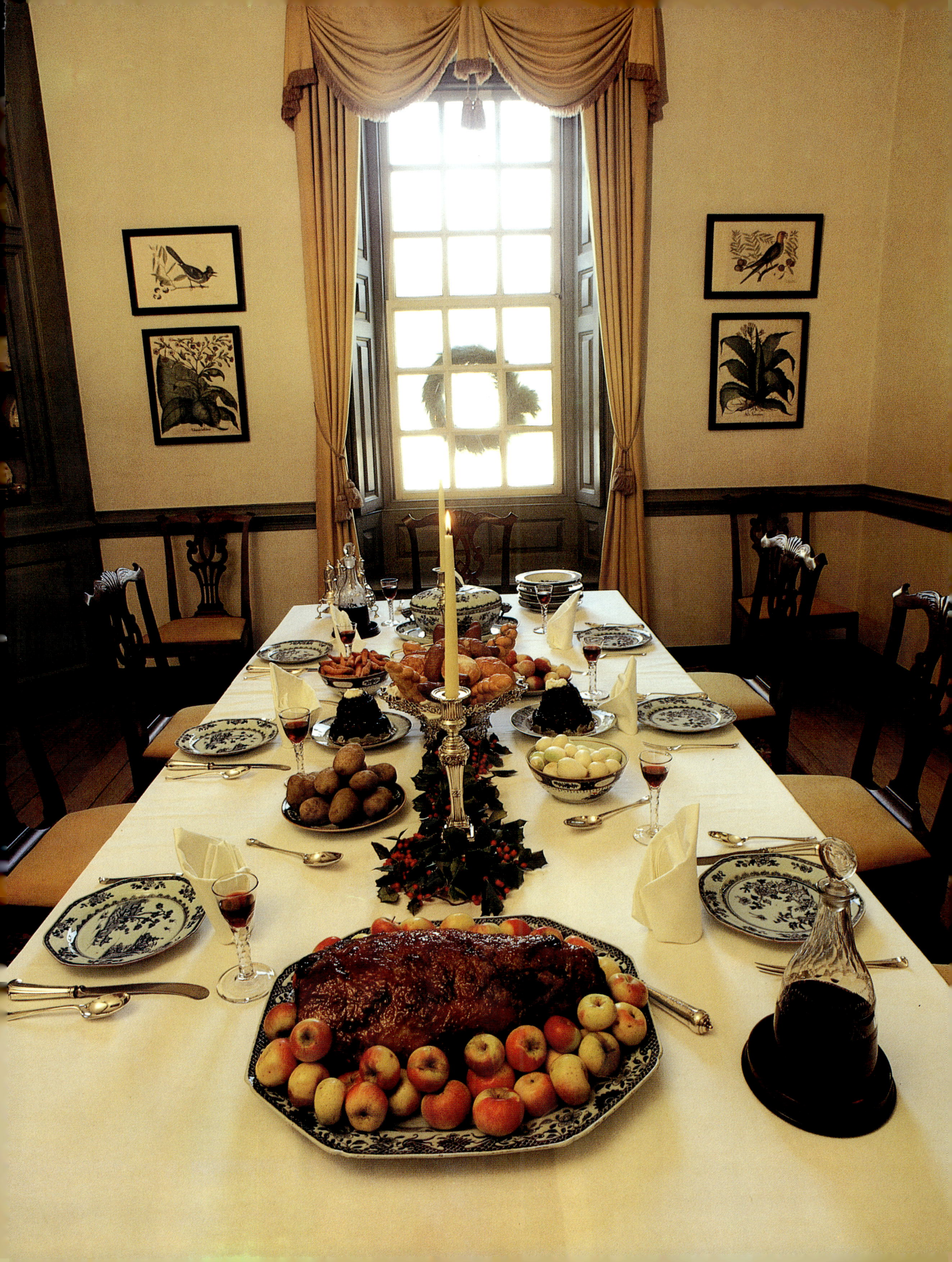

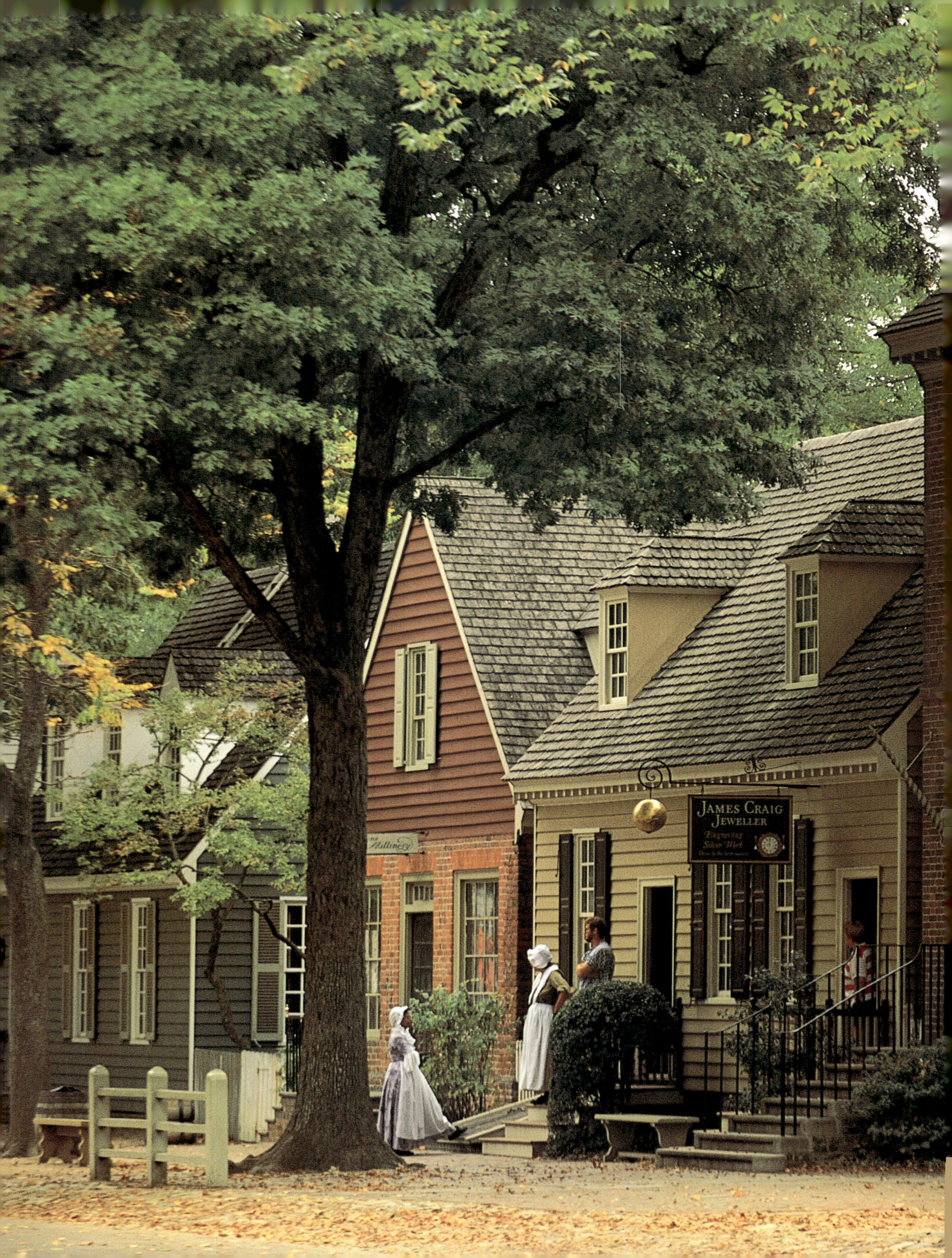
JAMES CRAIG
JEWELLER

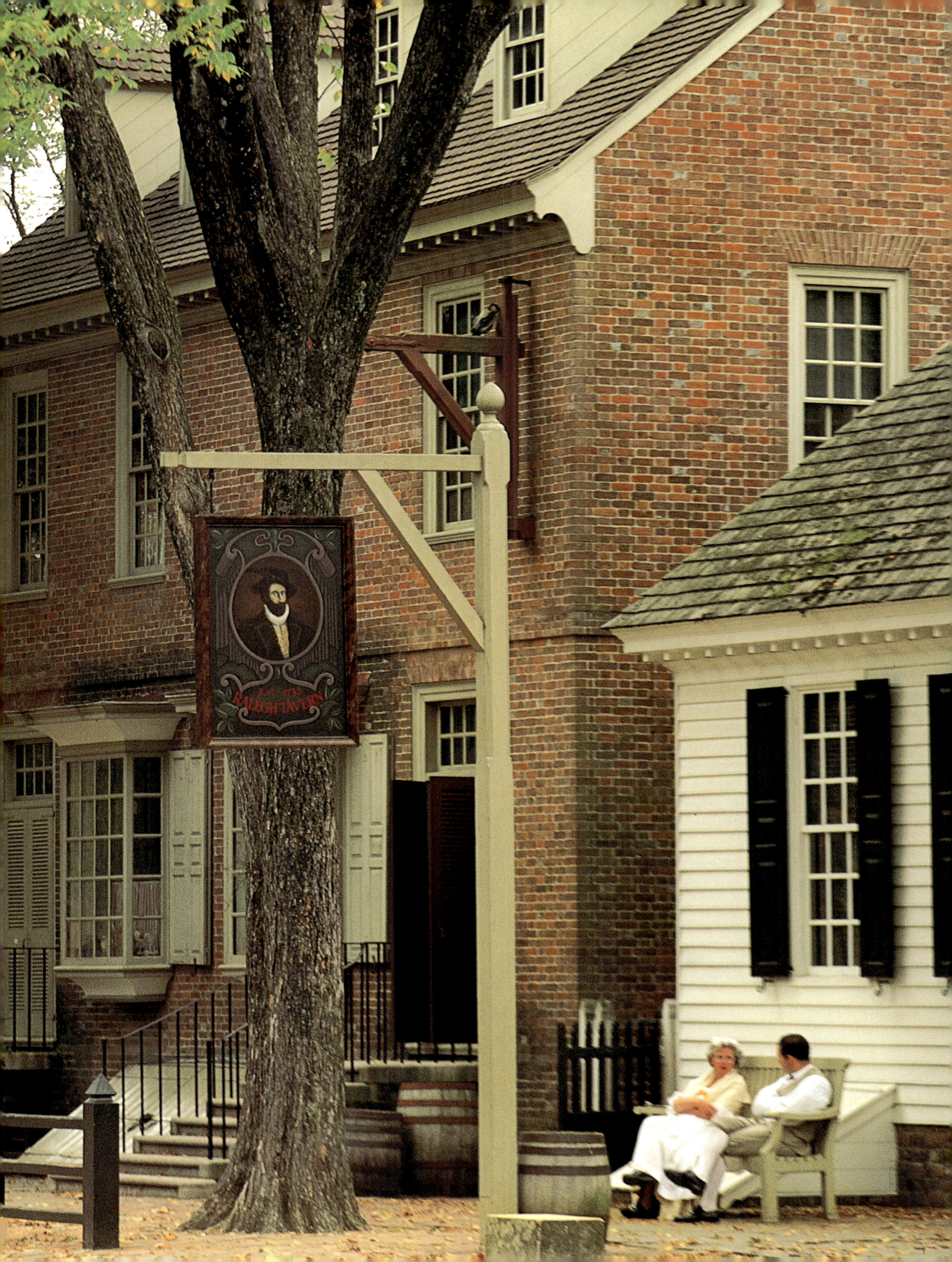

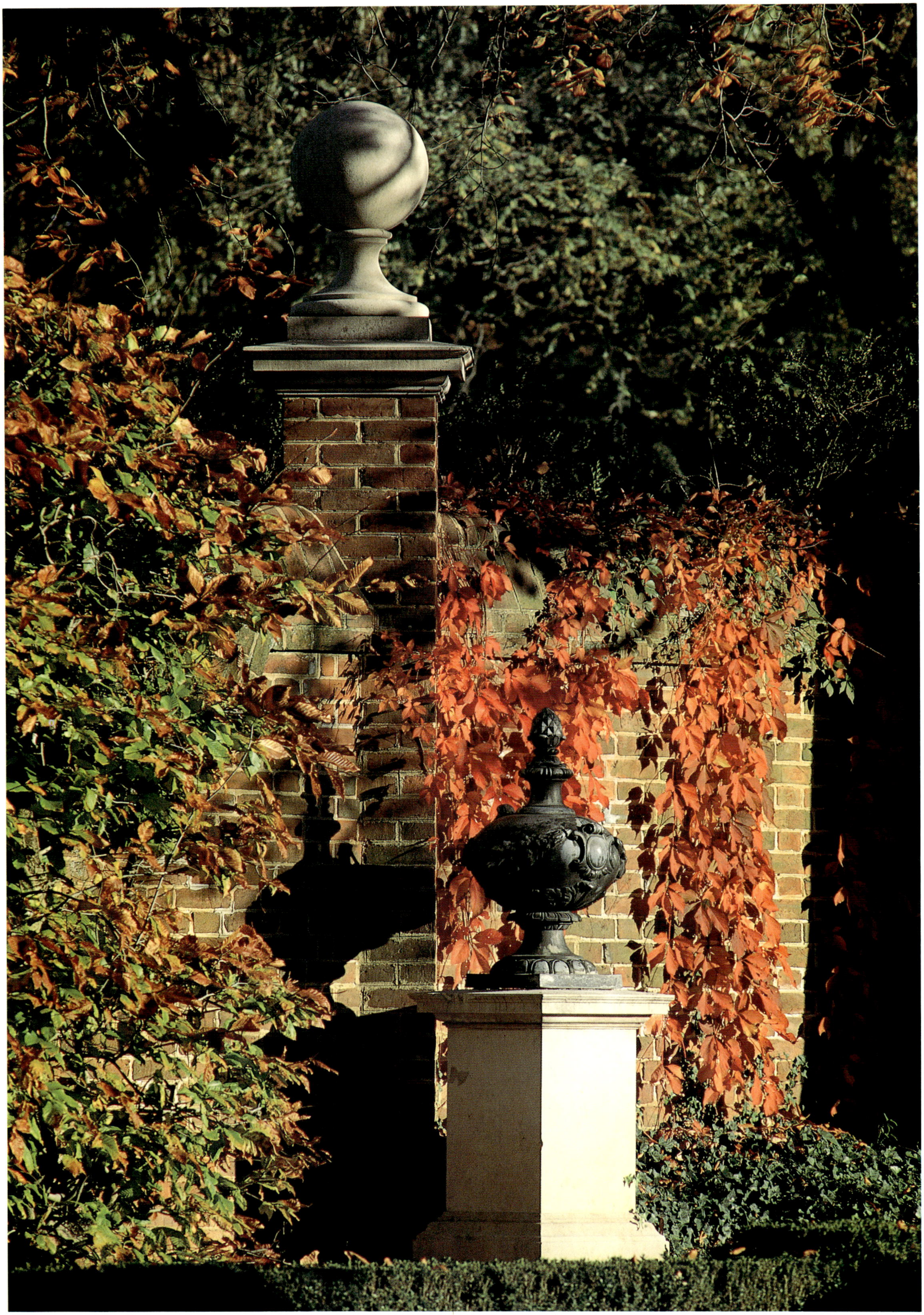

Pages 42 and 43: Raleigh Tavern, first built about 1717. Providing meals, drink, and lodging, taverns hosted councilors and burgesses, ship captains and lawyers, merchants and planters, who met within their doors to transact business, talk politics, and play cards.

Opposite: Urn in the Governor's Palace Ballroom Garden.

Above: A re-creation of a likely sign for Josiah Chowning's Tavern as it might have appeared in 1770.

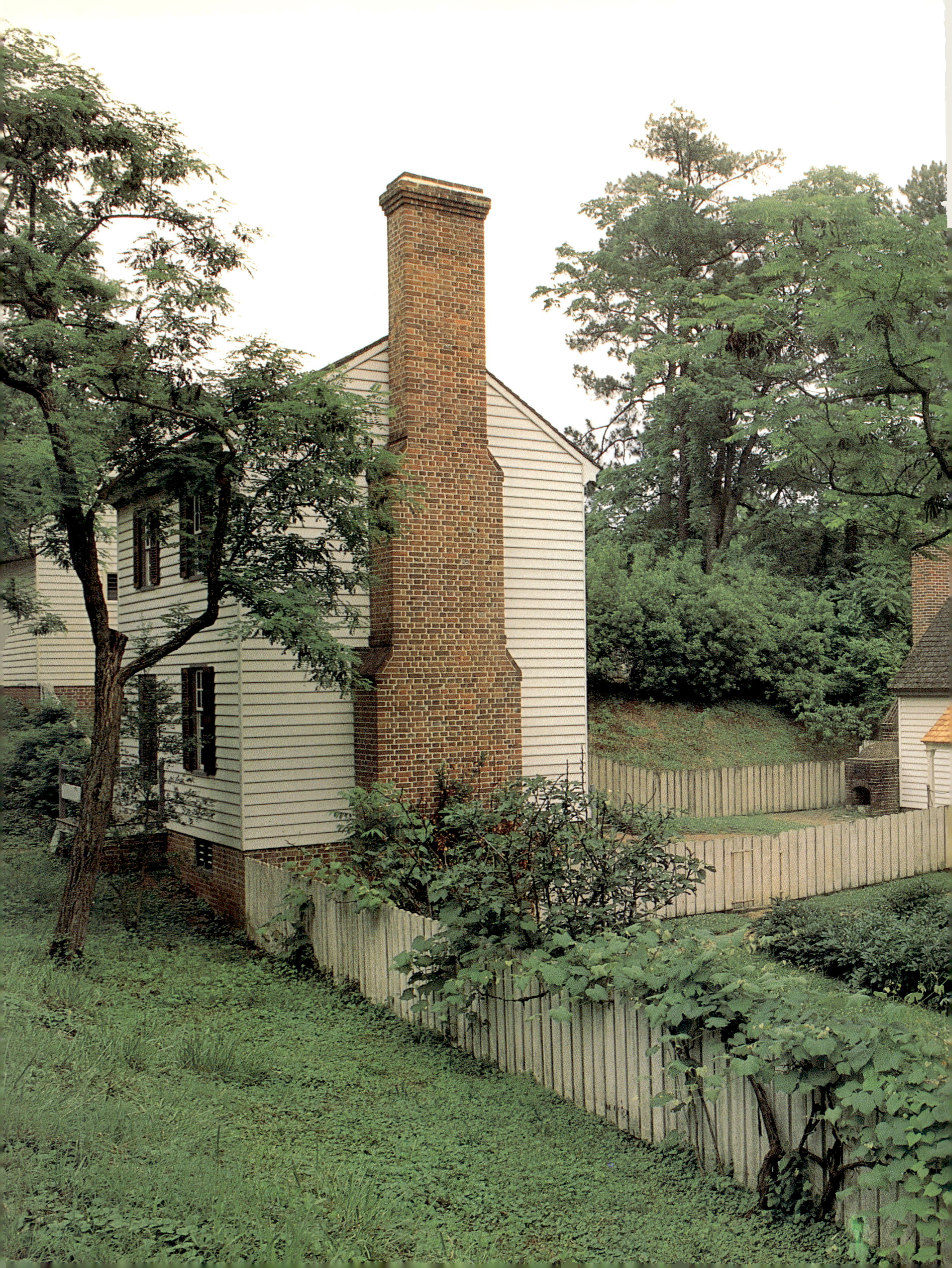

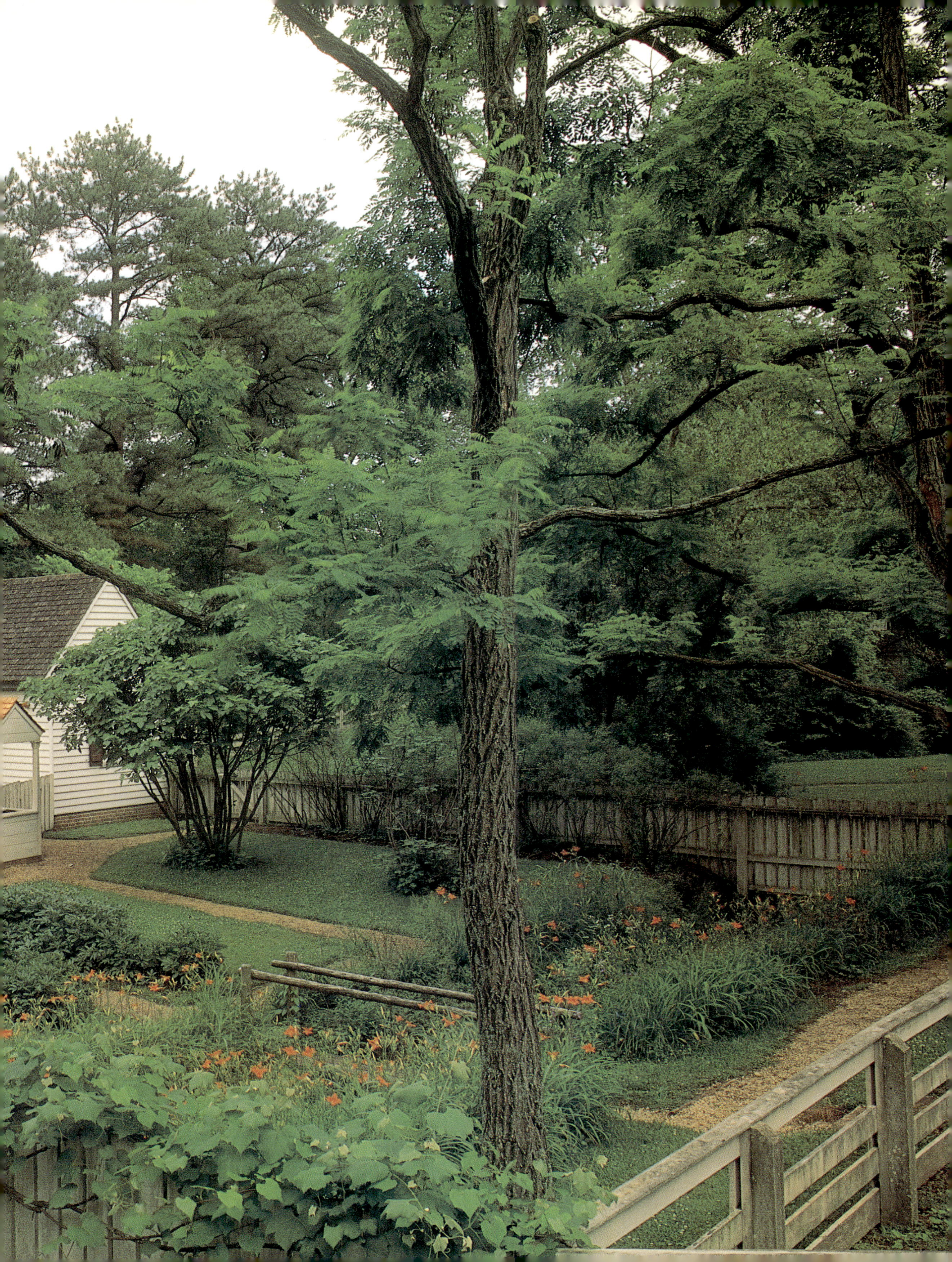

From the Church runs a Street northward called Palace Street; at the other End of which stands the Palace or Governor's House, a magnificent Structure, built at the publick Expense, finished and beautified with Gates, fine Gardens, Offices, Walks, a fine Canal, Orchards, &c...This likewise has the ornamental Addition of a good Cupola or Lanthorn, illuminated with most of the Town, upon Birth-Nights, and other Nights of occasional Rejoicings.

Reverend Hugh Jones
The Present State of Virginia, 1724

Pages 46 and 47: Colonial-style house and garden on Nicholson Street.

Opposite: A spectacular autumn at the Governor's Palace.

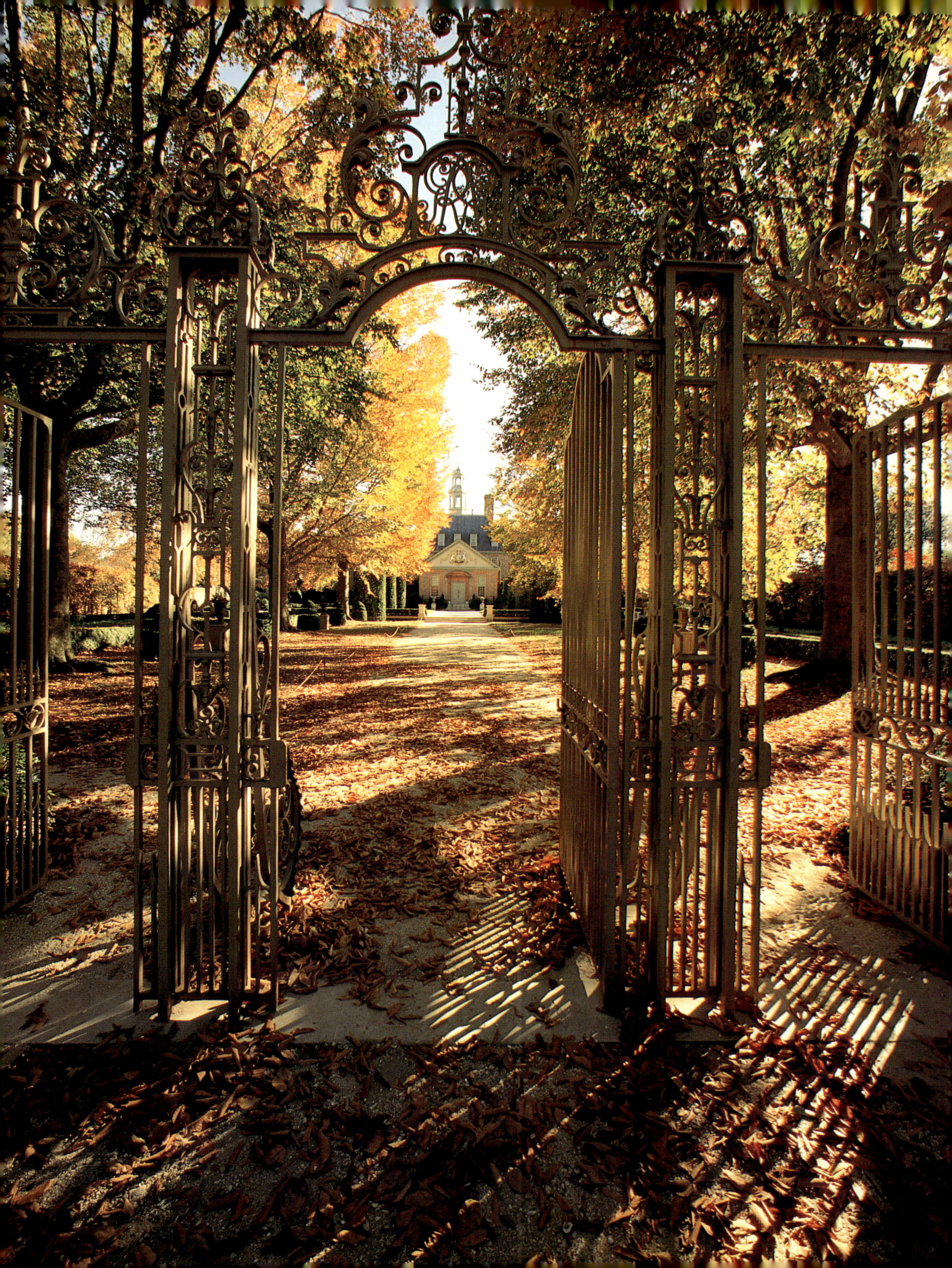

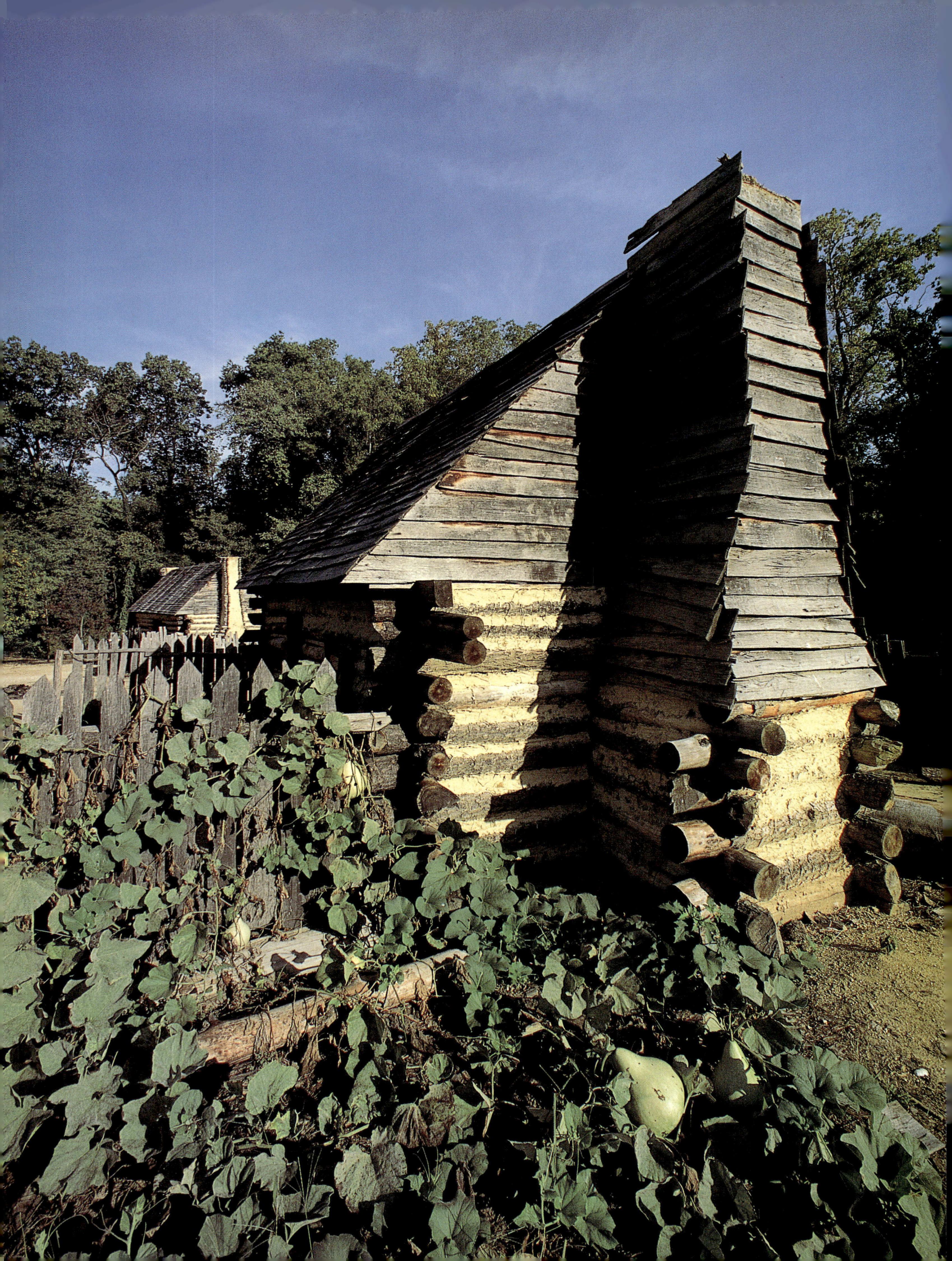

Slave quarters at Carter's Grove Plantation, built about 1750-55.

Domestic animals grazing in timeless scenes.

53

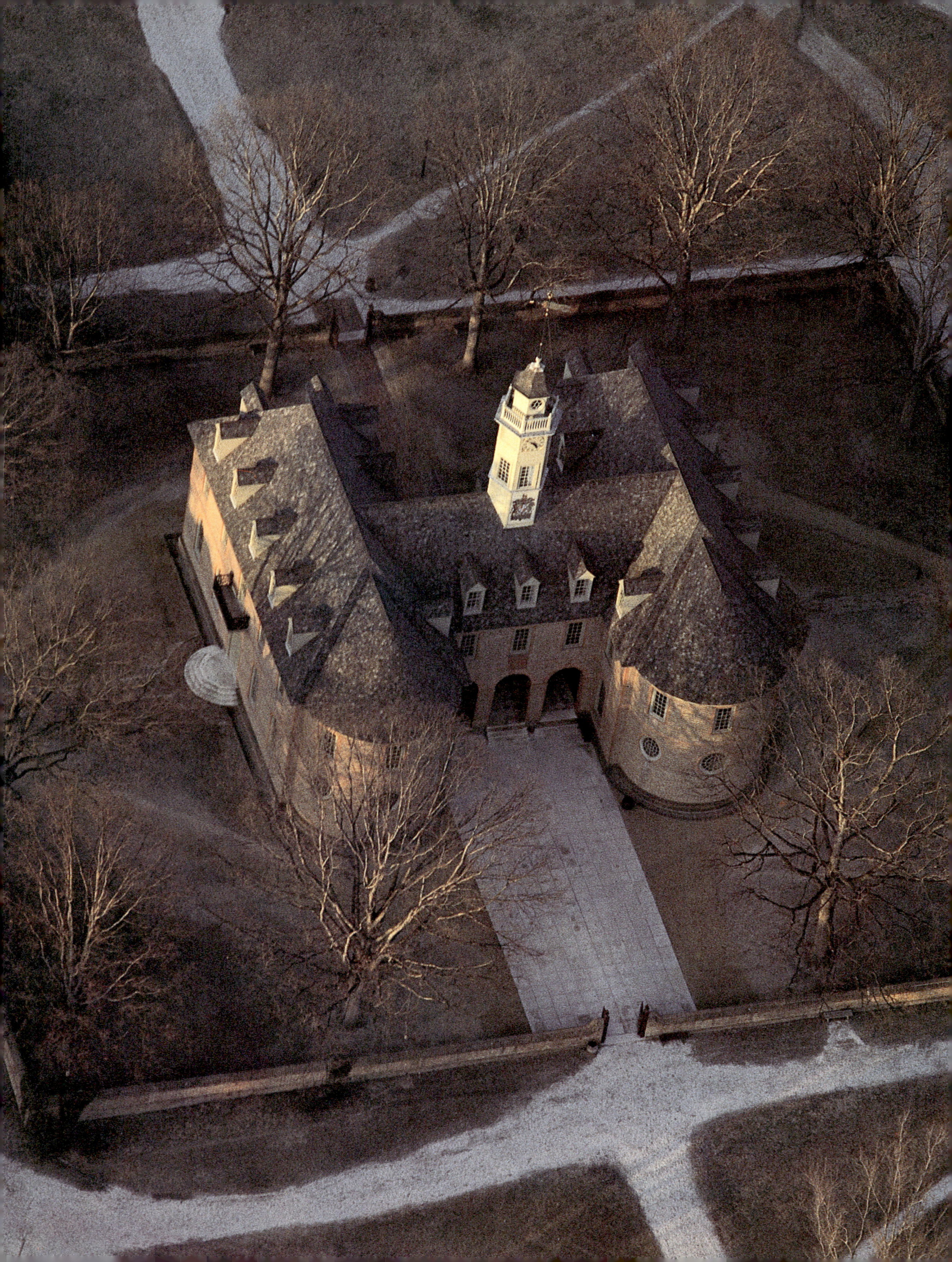

The Capitol Building is a reconstruction of the original 1705 building that burned in 1747.

Pages 56 and 57: Cannons by the Courthouse, and the Powder Magazine at Market Square. The Courthouse was built shortly before the Revolution.

At Colonial Williamsburg the past is authentically recalled.